HOW TO LAUNCH

A

BEST-SELLING

CHRISTIAN BOOK

Lorilyn Roberts
Best-Selling Author

How to Launch a Best-Selling Christian Book

TABLE OF CONTENTS

TABLE OF CONTENTS
(continued)

Prologue

I began the John 3:16 Marketing Network in the summer of 2010 and a year later we had grown to the point that I needed to compile the articles that I had written into one document. This e-book contains some of those articles as well as marketing suggestions for how to launch a book to best-seller status in categories and subcategories on Amazon. I have also included other information to help authors navigate through Amazon—helpful tidbits for implementing a successful book launch as well as building an Amazon platform.

As authors joined the John 3:16 Marketing Network, I was spending a great deal of time answering the same questions repeatedly. While the information is specifically directed towards helping authors in the network, this resource can be easily tailored to fit anyone's needs. Feedback from this book has been positive. Authors know what to expect once they join and the frequently updated information helps everyone to navigate through the steps of a successful book launch.

May you also find this book helpful and a blessing as you market your book.

Have questions? You can contact me on my website at http://lorilynroberts.com or via email at llwroberts at cox.net.

Chapter One
Novel Idea for Christian Marketing
The Very Unnovel Problem

"You are not famous. You are not an expert in any particular subject. You have no fancy initials after your name. **The reality is nobody cares about you or your book**."

As depressing as this might sound, I prefaced my presentation with these words to the First Coast Christian Writers in Jacksonville, Florida, in the fall of 2009, but I ended my comments with the following observation:

"If you were to present Jesus' marketing plan for the Gospel, it would probably go something like this: Jesus had no Internet, no television, no blog, no books, and no public relations people. All He had were twelve disciples whom He loved and on whom He had to depend to spread the Gospel around the world.

"God used those flawed human beings to bring 'The Greatest Story Ever Told' to a world way beyond what they could have envisioned, both then and into the future. If God can do that, our books can reach those for whom they were written. We don't need to overstretch our wallets, but neither should we sit idle. We should pray hard and seek His will not only in our writing, but also in our marketing. Ultimately, God will get our book into the hands of readers if we are good stewards of the gifts He's given us.

"I wonder what the marketing people would say today if we told them our marketing strategy was to have twelve people talk about our book to everyone they met and that was all. We had no money to spend either. This is just a thought to ponder as I think about how difficult it is to market."

On December 30, 2009, I wrote a blog, "Marketing a POD book in 2009: Reflections on What Worked and What Didn't." I shared what I had learned and my determination to "keep on keeping on" for what I believed God had called me to do—to market *Children of Dreams* the best way I knew how. I believed I had written a book that others would want to read if they knew about it. That is the key—and great obstacle for many Christian authors.

The John 3:16 Marketing Network emulates what Jesus taught His disciples, enabling them to share the Gospel despite persecution, opposition, and hardship. At its heart, the John 3:16 Marketing Network is one Christian author helping another Christian author, and ultimately, advancing HIS WORD around the world. Let me give some background about myself.

In 2009, I attended a well-known Christian writers' conference in Florida. Before the conference, I worked diligently to complete *Children of Dreams*, an inspirational and spiritual book about the adoption of my two daughters. Throughout the book, I compared their adoptions to God's adoption of us. I spent three months writing *Children of Dreams* and six months revising and editing it. An English major did the first bit of editing. The second round of editing was done by a high school English teacher. Then I had a professional editor who read it and loved it so much she critiqued it some more. She also gave me tips on how to improve my writing for the future. Before the final version was printed, I had a friend with a Ph.D. in communications take one last look. She offered a few more suggestions.

Twenty-two beta readers from different walks of life read *Children of Dreams*. Some I didn't know personally. Several volunteered when I asked for help from the church's reading group (which I had never attended). I begged some people. Some sweet souls offered to read *Children of Dreams* because they knew my children and wanted to read their adoption story.

All those who helped in the early drafts are acknowledged in the prologue section of the book. I graciously accepted the advice given and looked at every note and comment. I swallowed my pride and learned how much I didn't know, but I also realized how blessed I was to have so many willing to invest their precious time reading the pages.

To read and evaluate what you like and don't like takes time. I don't take it lightly when anybody gives me his thoughts, even when I don't agree. At least he is thinking and processing my words, and usually, if the comments are given in kindness, there is something I can use. I might dream up an idea I wouldn't have thought about otherwise.

After months of going through this process, spending a few hundred dollars making review copies, followed by additional editing, I believed I had a good book to present to an editor at the conference. I expected further revisions. I had attended this conference on three previous occasions and figured someone would recommend more changes. I even spent $50 and bought an e-book about proper etiquette at a writer's conference—to make sure my heart was right and I wasn't setting myself up for failure.

I sent my submission in ahead of time as per the requirements of the conference. The critiqued submissions from the editors were to be returned to the authors after lunch on Friday.

The conference started on Wednesday. Lunchtime arrived on the anticipated day and nervous participants lined up to receive their packages. Each person in front of me received his submission. The volunteer looked everywhere for mine but couldn't find it. She reassured me that some were still out and to check back later.

I did not receive my critiqued submission until the following day when I insisted they find it. I looked at the notes jotted down from an editor of a well-known publishing house. His only comment was: "This doesn't meet our needs. You might consider submitting to a magazine."

I walked away upset but kept it to myself. I was okay with the thought my book might not be what he wanted, but to tell me to submit it to a magazine was an insult. *Children of Dreams* was 235 pages filled with twists and turns and unbelievable complications. There was no way he could have read my submission and gotten that impression.

Because of the long delay in receiving it, there were no openings left to meet with another editor. I stared at the sheets with all the appointment slots filled. I wondered how I could have paid such a huge sum of money to attend the conference and invested so much emotionally into my book and then not even have an opportunity to meet with anyone. Devastation might come close to describing my emotions.

I scrambled around to sign up with editors and agents who had slots to open up when people scratched appointments. I eventually met with three agents and two editors. Each time after the perfunctory greeting, I showed the listener my completed and bound book (if you are not a published author, you must have a finished manuscript before an agent or editor will talk to you).

Two agents asked me, "Do you have a platform. Do you have a mailing list?"

"No, I don't have a platform. I do have a website, and I'm willing to do whatever you ask to get my book out there."

One agent replied, "Come back and see me when you have one thousand people on your email list." I thanked her.

Another agent told me to send him a proposal. I returned home and spent three weeks preparing a proposal and mailed it to him. He emailed me back to the effect, "I'm not sure when I'll get around to reading it. If you haven't heard from me in a month, ring me up." I never bothered.

During the conference I tried to show my book to anyone who would look at it. "Is it a memoir? Oh, nobody is publishing memoirs right now."

I'm glad that isn't a long tradition. Otherwise, my kids would never have known about the incredible Christian witness of such folks as George Mueller, Martin Luther, J. Hudson Taylor, George Elliott, Corrie ten Boom, John Wycliffe, John Huss, and Johannes Gutenberg. I felt the Red Sea parting in front of me when people thought my book was only a memoir.

I never liked it being identified that way because memoirs are usually about dead people, and I am still very much alive. Besides, anyone who read *Children of Dreams* would strongly attest to the fact it is far more than just a memoir. Far be it for me to convince someone of that, especially when no one wanted to read a word.

One blessed editor did give me "the time of day." He was someone I had met at a previous conference. I wasn't going to present it to him because I knew it wasn't the kind of material he was looking for, but I was discouraged. It turned out he was interested and even read a page or two. I felt like my year's labor was validated by someone who appreciated my passion. He ranks high in my opinion of what an editor should be.

When our time ended, I reached over to grab my book, but he asked if he could take it with him. I was thrilled. Although nothing ever materialized from that meeting, I later received a personal letter from the president of the organization thanking me for God's testimony in the lives of my family. It wasn't the endorsement I'd hoped for, but I appreciated the fact that he took the time to write me.

I returned home still determined to publish *Children of Dreams*. I had vowed early on not to use Print on Demand (I think the Bible says we shouldn't take vows). I had previously published an illustrated children's book, *The Donkey and the King*, POD, and while I never regretted it, I learned from that experience how difficult it is to market a POD book. I wanted *Children of Dreams* to "get out there" and receive the exposure it deserved.

I was also tired of the prejudice that POD authors receive. I wanted to be taken seriously. After all, I had done multiple rewrites and had many people read it. I had done everything I could humanly-speaking to make *Children of Dreams* one of those books that resonated with inspiration, hope, and redemption.

When I returned from the conference, I did not let my disillusionment with the Christian publishing world dissuade me from looking at the secular market. I went to the bookstore and bought one of those expensive marketing guides and searched for what was hot.

Unlike the Christian market, secular publishers were seeking memoirs and publishing them. As I methodically put together my list of possible publishers, I began to wonder, "Why am I doing this?"

I had to wait until summer to submit to XYZ Publishing Company. Another company only accepted submissions during the winter. As I examined the various requirements for submitting queries or manuscripts, my frustration mounted when it seemed like I couldn't submit *Children of Dreams* anywhere right away.

"Why don't I just POD publish it and work my behind off to market it?" I said one day. Besides, I'm fifty-four years old. I wrote *Children of Dreams* initially for my daughters. I wanted them to know what I went through to adopt them, and ultimately, to see God's hand in all of it. I wanted them to know it was God who brought them out of depravity to a new life where they would know love and security—and most of all—their Savior. While I spent years knocking on doors that might never open, I might die. Then they would never know their story.

I prayed about it because until this point, I was resistant to POD. Was it my pride? God made it clear to me to publish it POD. I have never regretted it. Not because I've sold tons of books—I haven't, but because God has taught me so much I would never have learned otherwise.

My book was published on April 30, 2009. If you read the article I posted in December 2009, I share some of the things that worked and didn't work. There were a lot of things that did nothing but cost a lot of money. I won't repeat them here (see my previous website reference).

I gathered reviews on Amazon and many other websites. As of this writing, I have eighty reviews on Amazon with a 4.6 star overall ranking. I received five stars from the Christian Book Review, Midwest Book Review, Allbooks Review, and the FaithWriters Seal of Approval for Outstanding Read.

While I was marketing *Children of Dreams*, I realized how much I loved what I was doing and enrolled in graduate school to work on my Masters in Creative Writing. I couldn't find a good local Christian critique group, so I started one. I feel blessed that someone was willing to help me in this endeavor.

Where there is a will, God provides the way. I continue to remind myself, I must be the best that I can be, not for my glory, but for the one who gives me the opportunity. To whom much is asked, much is given.

If you have read this far, I hope you will stick with me as I get to the heart of what I want to share next in "A Christian Marketing Twist on an Old Concept."

Chapter Two
A Christian Marketing Twist on an Old Concept

As I continued to market *Children of Dreams* and conversed with authors, I found I wasn't the only one walking this lonely road. Many Christian writers not yet discovered write with passion and gusto—books people would want to read if they knew about them.

It is overwhelming to navigate the web and figure out where to spend money prudently to achieve the best results. Boatloads of companies and individuals offer various packages. If you aren't discerning, you can invest a lot of money in strategies that may give you exposure but not generate sales. There is a difference. You can do a Google search of my name and easily pull up twenty pages. I no longer wanted just exposure. I wanted to sell more books.

I tried many things to increase sales. I suspect many give up believing it's too hard and too expensive. How many excellent books will never see the light of day? Even with lots of exposure, selling many books is tough. Sometimes I think authors spend so much time writing and promoting their own books that it doesn't allow enough time for them to appreciate what others are writing. Finding the right balance can be elusive.

One of my favorite Bible verses is Colossians 3:23: "Whatever you do, do your work heartily, as for the Lord rather than for men." You persevere, work hard to produce a product that others need or want, and eventually, if you are wise with the gifts God gives you, He will bless you.

With the downturn in the economy, marketing has become more difficult. I have less money to spend and so do the traditional publishing houses. Despite what the media says, that things are improving, I am not convinced. When I look at Europe, particularly Greece, Italy, Spain and Portugal, I don't see how we can escape the impact of their economic woes here in the U.S. and Canada. The reality is, Christian publishers must sell thousands of books by at least some of their authors to make a profit. If they don't, they won't stay in business. How are they going to divvy up the bulk of their funds for promotional purposes? As a business owner, I can tell you, it won't be for an unknown, unproven author.

When a traditional publishing company's agent asks me, **"How are you going to market your book?"** I understand how important it is to assure the editor I can be an asset and not a liability. Until recently, however, I was clueless how I could do it effectively. So are many others, and that's something I hope to change.

Recently I listened to a well-known Christian author compare POD publishing to traditional publishing. He discouraged writers from going the POD route, claiming that a person who publishes a POD book is not really an author. I wanted to tell him, the way marketing is today, it's almost impossible for someone like me to get traditionally published—without a platform and a lot of money, neither of which I have.

I came away discouraged feeling like a second-class author. It isn't enough to have a well-written book. The reality is, you could have a book as great as Charles Dickens's *Great Expectations* and the world might never know about it.

I have read articles, blogs, excerpts, and books by unknown authors. Wonderful stories abound in cyberspace. That's not to say mediocre writing doesn't grace the pages of hopeful aspirants, but can we not encourage each other and lend a helping hand? What is our ultimate goal? If God is all powerful, and I don't believe any Christian would deny that, He can get our books into the hands of those who will appreciate them and buy them. If anything, I think we tend to limit what God can do because our expectations are too low. We have an awesome God who is in the business of doing the impossible.

The other day I was on a Christian writers' website. The blog mentioned how long it takes an unknown writer to get his book published by a traditional publisher—seven years. If I had dutifully followed the trail blazed by others before me, *Children of Dreams* wouldn't be out into the marketplace until I was sixty years old (ouch, that hurts).

I will compare that to my former husband's educational experience. I put him through medical school, which took four years. His residency following that took four more years. In eight years, he went from building bikes for minimum wage at Toys R Us to treating cancer patients making hundreds of thousands of dollars. If the universities can accomplish that, surely there is something the Christian publishing world can do to make that seven-year process go a little faster. After all, we aren't training to become brain surgeons.

Let me tell a little bit more about myself. I am a single mother with two daughters (fourteen and twenty-one). I'm employed full time as a closed captioner for television. I just completed my Masters in Creative Writing. I lead a local Christian writers critique group (Word Weavers) in Gainesville that meets once a month. We have four neurotic cats and two wacky dogs. That in itself is enough to keep me busy.

On top of that, living is stressful—paying bills, cooking, laundry, running my fourteen-old daughter everywhere (she's a level eight gymnast who spends twenty hours a week at a gym forty-five minutes away), plus I am committed to a church, attend weekly, and am involved in a small group that meets once a week for prayer. I also try to exercise on a regular basis (I want to be around for my grandkids). I am not complaining. God has blessed me with more than I could possibly do in my own strength.

My point is, in order to fit it all in, I must work efficiently and maintain an attitude that brings glory to God. Otherwise, I will receive the praise of man and not my heavenly Father.

I believe Christian marketing is one of the most inefficient enterprises in existence. The way some of it is done now, I wonder if it's working at all. Or I could loosely quote James Scott Bell, "Only twenty percent of marketing works; the trouble is, we don't know which twenty percent."

Let me digress and make one more comparison, and then I will get on to my novel idea.

In February, I received an invitation from Steve Harrison to enroll in a class called "How to Make Your Book an Almost Instant Best Seller and Sell Tons of Copies—Even if You're a Marketing Novice."

Steve Harrison is a guru in Internet marketing. He occasionally will have a free webinar where he will feature a guest promoting some aspect of writing or marketing. I had attended a few in the past—I like free things, especially when I don't have to go anywhere—and so I signed up for this one.

The guest on his show was Peggy McColl, an author who's had many bestsellers. I listened to the seminar and was intrigued. She explained how anyone could take any book and make it a bestseller on Barnes & Noble or Amazon by following a few prescribed things exactly. It didn't have to be a new book. It could be an older book. It could be fiction. It could be nonfiction.

I have sold most of my books on Amazon so this was attractive to me (I was never able to get *Children of Dreams* in bookstores even though I paid money to provide a restocking expense if any books were returned).

What impressed me most about the Bestseller Coaching Program, however, was they guaranteed success if you followed all the steps in the program. I had told myself (and God) I would no longer pay for any marketing programs unless they came with a guarantee—literally. This program came with a one hundred percent guarantee.

To enroll in the Bestseller Coaching Program is not cheap. It cost me $2,500. I would have to sell dozens of books to recoup the money, but if I sold enough books to make *Children of Dreams* number one, that would make me a bestselling author on Amazon. I figured I would do whatever was required to make it work. If I failed, then I would get my money back.

I was in the middle of my screenwriting course in February, March, and April, so I knew it would have to wait a little while, but the guarantee ran for a year. That also sounded good, so I signed up for it.

There were many others participating in the Bestseller Coaching Program, and we had a group that agreed to mentor each other as we launched our books. I have received emails from some of them, and I asked, since I had not started my campaign, "How is it going?" Everyone responded saying the hardest part was getting people to support their "campaign."

Let me explain a little bit about how the Bestseller Coaching Program works. The idea behind it is you have a launch date, and you direct people to Amazon or Barnes & Noble to buy your book. You do this basically in two ways. First, you get Joint Venture Partners to promote your book through an email to their clients on the day of your book launch. The idea is to have everybody know about your book and buy it on the designated date. You add value to those buying your book by enlisting partners that will be willing to offer bonus gifts during that 24-hour period. The basic premise of the program resonated with what I knew worked.

My parents own a small map company in Atlanta. Each summer they solicit orders for the new Aero Atlas to be published in the fall. Customers can buy the book map at a discounted price until September when the price increases, so it creates a sense of urgency. If the customer wants to receive his new map at the discounted rate, he has to buy it within the timeframe given. Each client is contacted individually—the emphasis being on customer service.

I spent several summers as a teenager working in the business, making phone calls, and encouraging each customer to buy his map at the lower price, emphasizing how many new streets had been added. Surely he wanted to locate his customers more efficiently without wasting precious time and gas. That would increase his profit margin.

Fast forward about thirty years. I provide closed captioning for television. One of the channels that I captioned until recently is QVC. QVC is the guru of home shopping with its own network. The Q stands for quality, the V stands for value, and the C stands for customer service. One of QVC's most successful marketing strategies is the "Today's Special Value." Each day QVC presents a product at midnight. I used to caption the 12-1 a.m. time slot so I saw it routinely in action. The Today's Special Value is a spiffed-up, brand-spanking new product that will make your life easier, better, or something you believe you can't live without.

Sometimes it's jewelry. At other times it is clothing. Many times it's electronics—the newest gadgets in cameras, TVs, or computers; or maybe it is a kitchen product (yes, I bought a bunch of kitchen absurdities).

However, besides presenting an excellent product (you must have that to start with), as a Christian, we shouldn't accept anything less), there are several other factors that enable QVC to sell hundreds or thousands of a particular item in a short span of time.

First, there is a sense of urgency. The tagline could be something like, "You shouldn't wait or it might sell out. Then you won't be able to purchase it."

Oftentimes it's a version of something you can't get anywhere else. Perhaps a new style purse that might be in an unusual or different color; maybe it's a two-for-one pineapple slicer. There are many variations on this concept.

Another example would be the Keurig coffee maker I bought. They added in extra K-cups worth about $20 as well as some other online freebies (which I never bothered to get). However, the extra K-cups were used and I felt like I received a lot of value for my money.

That's what we want to create when we sell something. We want the buyer to be convinced he has gotten a bargain. The only catch is he has to buy the product when we want him to buy it.

I would be amused when QVC had the cleaning experts on. They loved their mops and microfiber pads about as much as I love my Bible; and passion sells. As authors, if we can't be passionate about our words and willing to market our book with that much zest, then maybe we should find something else to do.

On many occasions QVC devoted a significant amount of time to something I could not have cared less about—maybe the newest version of a popular screwdriver or wrench. Of course, I would rather be captioning baseball anyway, but by the end of the presentation, I would be embarrassed to admit how many times I was cajoled into buying something I never knew I needed.

While not everything in the above examples applies to selling a book, the concept does. I knew the Bestseller Coaching Program would work if enough Joint Venture Partners could be brought on board. I've had several conversations with authors who have launched their Bestseller Campaign and the one comment I've heard is it's very hard to get people to help you. Some don't see the value. Others are busy and don't respond back.

I surmised this might be the weakest link in the marketing program. One author told me for every twenty people she contacted, she received one response. That means to convince two hundred people to partner with her on her book launch, she would need to contact four thousand people.

As I thought about this, I remembered a comment a Christian author recently made to me: Writing is done alone, but you can't get anywhere in this business as far as publishing without help from others. It's impossible.

God did not intend for us to be loner Christians. He wants us to be involved in a church and reach out to others as part of the Body of Christ. The Gospel of John tells us, as paraphrased in a song by Jars of Clay, "They will know we are Christians by our love."

Chapter Three
The Nuts and Bolts of a Book Launch

We write what the world needs to hear even if they don't know it. We have a story to tell and the world will literally go to hell if we don't pen or type it (lest you think I exaggerate, I was saved by reading the Gospel of Matthew and not from someone witnessing to me).

In a sense, we are missionaries, and there is plenty of soil to be tilled, planted, and harvested. We don't know when the Lord's return will be, but I believe we can publish and get books into the marketplace far more efficiently by joining together and helping each other to achieve success.

Christians help each other in various ways in the publishing and marketing world. Relationships are built over time and meaningful connections forged. What if we had a dynamic group that would link Christian writers together and help them to launch their books? Suppose we took the model that the Bestseller Coaching Program uses in the secular world and applied it to Christian authors? Could we shorten the length of time it takes an unpublished author to get published from seven years down to two years or even one?

The John 3:16 Marketing Network. came into being from these early musings. Even the name emphasizes the Christ-centeredness of the group. Today we have two hundred fifty plus members. We have a blog with all the members listed and a link to author websites. In 2013, I plan to have a regular schedule for blog postings featuring top authors and marketers. One of my goals is for the John 3:16 Marketing Network Blog to become one of the top Christian writing and marketing blogs on the web.

First, let me give a brief overview of how a launch takes place and later I will get into more specifics. When we launch a new book, John 3:16 authors send out Facebook and Tweet announcements and many host the launching author on his or her blog. Some authors in the network will have reviewed the author's new book.

How can this be helpful for an author when attending a writer's conference? Let's take my example and what could have taken place instead of what actually did. I present *Children of Dreams* to an editor. Instead of being asked, "Do you have a platform? How are you going to market your book? Do you have a thousand email subscribers?" The editor can focus on whether my book is something he would be interested in publishing. Is *Children of Dreams* the type of book his boss could get excited about?

Think of all the advantages the John 3:16 Marketing Network offers. The traditional publisher has more options. There are more authors to choose from and more creative ideas for both fiction and nonfiction books. Publishers don't have to be as concerned about the bottom line, knowing a group of Christian authors will help promote the author's book. The publishing company can be assured that the author, as part of the John 3:16 Marketing Network, will have help launching his book using a proven, successful method.

Today we have authors, known and unknown; publishing companies; and even marketing gurus. All participants look to the John 3:16 Marketing Network to promote their books—both POD published authors and mainstream authors. I believe God has given each author a unique story. I don't see myself in competition with anyone else. Maybe this is too simplified, but why should I be jealous of someone else's success? He is promoting the Gospel at some level if he is a Christian author, and for that, I can rejoice.

A traditional publisher is assured no matter who the author is, there is a network of authors behind the book, helping to get a book noticed as a top-seller on Amazon. A top ranking on Amazon and Barnes & Noble is one of the pathways to a "New York Times" bestseller.

In no way does this lessen the responsibility of the author marketing his book. Instead, it puts him at the forefront of efforts as the "director." He must initiate the contact with other authors, take the time to research prospective authors, and be familiar with the types of books or articles they write. Within a Christian framework, authors understand how it works and are willing to be a part of a network to help a fellow Christian author.

Both POD authors and traditionally published authors are networked in the John 3:16 Marketing Network. The mode of publication is irrelevant as far as promotion. For example, perhaps an author is publishing a father's book of poetry or a child's book of short stories; maybe a person only wants a few copies of a family genealogy; or perhaps someone needs a book done quickly for a particular event. Or suppose someone felt God was leading him to publish a book POD for reasons we may never know. Should we tell him what he is doing has no value? Or silently think his way is inferior to our way? Who are we to question what God has told someone else to do? In my experience, God oftentimes does things in what humanly speaking could be called "irrational."

The list goes on and on for whether a book should be published POD or traditionally. The John 3:16 Marketing Network has come together to help both. I hope the Christian publishing world can choose to embrace those who labor over the written word in whatever form it's ultimately presented. As far as I can tell, both methods are here to stay. It is harder now than it was twenty years ago to do things the way they have always been done with traditional publishing. I don't expect that to change. I sense it will get harder.

My goal has been realized in the John 3:16 Marketing Network. POD and traditionally published authors have come together to help each other. Each has its place in the market and serves a specific purpose. In whatever way those words are printed, the focus and question should always be: Are we doing everything we can to promote our books to a secular, humanistic world that needs more Christian literature?

Joining together in a Christian Marketing Network has worked for both. To say it another way, the John 3:16 Marketing Network has become a win-win for all authors. Traditional publishing companies love to have a top-selling author garner many authors to partner with him on his book launch. Even without being a well-known author, using the strategies emphasized by the network and through networking, a POD author can and has promoted his or her book on many occasions and made it a bestseller.

Examples of this in other areas of life abound. Look at all the Christian organizations that help those in need. Two of my favorites are World Vision and Samaritan's Purse. The John 3:16 Marketing Network has members from all over the world who converse with each other on a daily basis.

Amazon and Barnes & Noble make no distinction between Christian and non-Christian books or any other kind of book as far as placement on their websites. It boils down to book sales. The John 3:16 Marketing Network has helped many authors with publicity and promotional opportunities, and the biggest winner has been the public. With our help on book launches, authors have obtained higher sales rankings than they would have received otherwise. In the end, we have given Christian authors more opportunity to share the Gospel. My ultimate goal is to see Christian books ranked in the top ten on Amazon. Why not change the world one book at a time as Biblical principles and values dominate the bestseller lists?

The John 3:16 Marketing Network is made up of Christian authors helping each other to launch books. The network has enabled all of us to make better use of limited time and money as we combine our resources to promote each other in a meaningful and loving way.

Even recently in the news, there are examples of the value of networking. The merger of Continental and United Airlines helped both companies to survive in a difficult market through combining resources. In the Christian publishing world, we have an opportunity not as competitors but as part of a "Body of Christian Writers."

In the two and a half years of our existence, we have helped unknown authors to receive more exposure than they would have received otherwise. The market is big enough and the opportunities are greater than ever—but with more opportunities come greater challenges. The only way to succeed is to be proactive and creative.

In March, 2013, we totally revamped how we are doing launches. With the advent of many free e-books available in Amazon's Kindle Direct Publishing (known as KDP Select) as well as Smashwords, we are integrating free and paid books in our book launches to give readers more choices and more exposure to great Christian books.

Again, the John 3:16 Marketing Network has proven one thing: Christian authors, through love and commitment, can work together to help each other launch books. A few years ago, many questioned if it could be done. Traditions die hard, but more than ever, Christian authors are striking out and self-publishing their books, many with great success.

I want to emphasize as a network, we seek the highest quality from all authors. The John 3:16 Marketing Network insists on it. If a member reads another author's work and feels it isn't something he can support, he needs to be upfront about it and let the author know. The author then needs to hire an editor to fix those problems. Lots of help by others can't salvage a poorly written book. As in any free market system, the best will survive and even excel; those that are inferior won't.

Today the John 3:16 Marketing Network has expanded into other areas. The element of trust is high among members. We value each other's input about book covers and contests and reviews and a host of other topics that get discussed on the John 3:16 forum.

Sometimes I think the heart of the Gospel is one beggar helping another beggar to know the Lord's unfathomable grace. It keeps me humble and relying on God to accomplish His sovereign purposes, knowing the outcome is in His hands. For that, I am grateful, especially in the writing arena.

This was my original vision for the John 3:16 Marketing Network. It's amazing to me how the vision God gave me two years ago so closely parallels what exists today. If you are interested in becoming a part of the John 3:16 Marketing Network or have any suggestions, please share them with me. Talk about my idea with others. Check out our blog. Drop me a comment at llwroberts@cox.net. I look forward to hearing from you. I am thankful God has helped so many authors to sell more books with the networking of John 3:16 authors. We have impacted the world for Christ and increased our literary influence on the world as Christian authors.

What can you expect to receive upon joining? We are always trying new things, but here is a list of some activities to pique your interest:

1. A network of Christian authors who will encourage you.
2. Access to the forum where you must be a member to post.

3. Support for putting together a book launch, including many members of the network tweeting about your launch. A fully prepared book launch site to make your book look good. You can visit our new launch site at http://John316marketingnetwork.com. All technical and professional expertise is provided for showcasing your book.

4. "How do I" tutorials available at http://bit.ly/11VKjcZ, along with links to other information.

5. Upcoming seminars by Sandra Beckwith.

6. Book reviewers.

7. Wealth of knowledge from uploaded files on the forum.

8. Opportunities to participate in future book anthologies (see our *Taste and See First Chapters* book on Amazon for an example of one we have already done).

9. Cross-promotional opportunities with fellow authors in the network (e.g., blog hop).

10. Opportunity to display the John 3:16 Marketing Network banner on your blog.

11. Professional marketing and editorial services at reduced cost to members (sometimes free when linked to promotions).

12. Access to John 3:16 beta readers from a pool of over three hundred readers.

13. Prayer support from members.

Chapter Four
The John 3:16 Marketing Network
Revolutionizes Christian Book Marketing
A Dream is Born

My doorbell rings.

"Mommy, it's UPS," my daughter hollers from the other room.

I'm glued to my chair captioning live television.

"Can you get it, honey?" I holler back.

The front door slams followed by the tearing of cardboard. My heart thumps faster than it has in a long time. My fingers sweat on the stenograph machine as I write 260 words per minute. My body succumbs to a supernova hot flash as I wait...and wait a few more seconds until a commercial break.

"Mommy, it's your book, and it's beautiful."

I must keep captioning until the next commercial break. Finally, the talking heads stop and I turn around. There it is—my daughter hands me my labor of love. I forget the late nights working instead of sleeping, the fast food at McDonald's to save time cooking, and the piled up laundry in the closet.

What is it like to hold your book for the first time and flip through the pages? If you are a published author, you know. You feel like you just gave birth—indeed, you have.

You send out a flurry of copies to your family, friends, and share your excitement with everyone with whom you come into contact. You learn how to check your rankings on Amazon and discover your book is rated in the top twenty in two subcategories. You wonder when you will get your first royalty check; and how many books have you sold in the first two weeks anyway?

A month later, the excitement wanes as you see your rankings plummet, you have run out of people you know who want to buy your book, and you can't afford to give away any more copies.

Now what? The hard work of marketing begins. You must stretch your horizon further than you could possibly imagine. You discover that while writing a book is hard, marketing is even harder. Should you invest the little money you have left to hire a publicist, or pay for a professional email campaign? Should you skimp on the money and just lick lots of stamps for library mailings—or what about the big bucks for radio and TV appearances? You manage to drum up a few public appearances close by and sell quite a few books in the process, but you can't travel far because you need that day job to pay your bills.

If any of this sounds familiar, know you are not alone. Most of us have tried some if not all of these things and probably dozens more.

One day my floundering marketing efforts took me on a different path. I was listening to a one-hour marketing seminar about how to become a best-selling author on Amazon or Barnes & Noble.

My dream was born. I said to myself, "I can do this." As I was contemplating how to begin, God refined my dream by giving me a vision beyond anything I could have imagined. The more I thought about it, the more I became convinced that God was leading me to try something new—something which had never been done in marketing. Why not have a network of Christian authors to help each other launch books? Why not try to make bestsellers of as many books with a Christian worldview as possible?

Dreams don't happen without a lot of hard work. To make it a reality, I needed authors who were willing "to give it a go."

I wrote a series of articles and contacted Christian authors on Facebook and other social networking sites. Slowly, I built a base of somewhat skeptical but entrepreneurial-type authors. Two months later, in October of 2010, we went live with the John 3:16 Marketing Network and launched our first book, *I'm a Keeper*, by Ray Lincoln, to best-seller status in multiple categories.

Since that time, I have been blessed to meet on our forum some of the most caring, dynamic, hard-working, educated, and talented authors in the industry. I wanted to share some of their unedited comments and hope that you, too, if you are a Christian author, will catch a glimpse of the potential we have to impact the underpinnings of Internet book marketing.

"Thanks to Lorilyn and all our fellow writers, this network has grown significantly. I agree with Mary Jo that our network will affect the future of Christian publishing. I personally am very grateful for all your helpful advice, prayers and just good 'virtual' company."—Fr Serafim – author, Carnival

"Although the Network was in its infancy when we did our launch, I am sure that it was a significant part of our success with hitting Bestseller in 5 Amazon.com categories. The people we are connecting with are becoming friends even though we have never met face-to-face. I firmly believe this group can have a great impact on the Christian book market."—Ray Lincoln – author, I'm a Keeper.

"The John 3:16 Book Marketing Network has been a God catalyst for so many talented authors here. I have not had the opportunity to enjoy the book launch benefits as mine is already in print (2009) - but I have made some wonderful contacts here and you have blessed me with your unwavering devotion to this group and its success. Your heavenly concept for this network has certainly been a blessing to so many - you are loved much Lorilyn!"—Deborah McCarragher – author, Mission Possible.

"Having the connection with fellow authors in John 3:16 gave me the confidence to pursue marketing with more passion, knowing I have the support of such loving friends.

"But what I value most is Lorilyn's willingness to go out of her way to help us out. Her constant support as she brings new ideas, offers new outlets, and points to specific marketing paths.

"Thank you so much, Lorilyn."—Janet Perez Eckles – author, Trials for Today, Treasure for Tomorrow and Simply Salsa: Dancing without Fear at God's Fiesta.

"What John3:16 has meant to me has been a renewal in my draggin' career. I have made some pretty neat contacts and met some lovely people. I've learned a lot about effective marketing at online retailers and feel like I've been helpful in encouraging and promoting and using my growing skills with other members of the group."—Lisa Lickel – author, Meander Scar.

To lose the lonely feeling, all I have to do is log on and look at my email and there have been things going on with the group to catch up on or prayer requests. It is just wonderful to know that I have that support group behind me for when I want to talk, need prayer, have something to share, or when I do a launch in the future. Thank you, Lorilyn, for introducing all of us."—Ashley Wintters – author, Shadows From the Past and Shadows of Suspicion.

"The John 3:16 Network has been fantastic in so many ways. First, through the expertise and guidance of those 'in the know,' my book MY MOTHER THE MAN-EATER reached best-seller status on Amazon.ca in the romance contemporary category, and stayed there for three days. This is something I never would have been able to achieve without the network. Secondly, this network is very supportive in more ways than just marketing. When like-minded people of faith gather together, a sense of mutual support and concern builds. I am thankful for that. John 3:16 was truly inspired and I thank Lorilyn Roberts for taking her vision and making it a reality."—Tracy Krauss – author, My Mother the Man-Eater and The Beat Goes On.

Writing and marketing our works can be a lonely enterprise, but it doesn't have to be. The John 3:16 Marketing Network enables me to gather wisdom from many authors who've been there and done that. Thus, I save time, money and frustration by crowd sourcing issues rather than depending upon my limited experiences. Solomon advised us that success and victory result from consulting many counselors. This network gives me an easy way to access these counselors."—Steve Miller – author, Enjoy Your Money! How to Make It, Save it, Invest It and Give It, and Sell More Books.

In the lonely world of writing, this network has provided encouragement, information and friendship with writers of many different genres. At a time of great changes in publishing when many are turned away from publication because the bigger companies are "full for the year," John 3:16 offers a variety of choices for authors to learn about non-traditional venues of seeing their writing in print and available to be read by others. It can give hope when others only discourage.—Elaine Cooper – author, The Road to Deer Run.

The John 3:16 Network has taught me a lot about the Kindle market and other technical issues with Amazon. I have come to know other authors' work and feel really blessed in reading their books. I was also able to get help in finding the right person in regards to the making of the video of my book and finding somebody to help me with my drawing. The interview with Donald Parker was amazing. Most *importantly, the encouragement, mutual support, and guidance from everybody has been tremendous.—Sana Edoja – author, Loving God.*

I would also add that many authors, after writing their first book, want to write another and another and another...

Chapter Five
The Finest Example of Launching Christian Books in the World
Q and A

I started the John 3:16 Network in the summer of 2010. Two years later, I am excited about what God is doing. I will share some Q&A that people often ask.

Question: I don't have a blog/website, don't use Twitter, and don't care for Facebook, but can I still be in the network? I have a book coming out that I need help promoting.

Answer: You must have an active blog or website to be a member of the John 3:16 Marketing Network. The reasons relate to the type of social marketing and network promotions we do.

You need a blog/website to help others if you wish to be a blog host for a launch. It shows you have enough knowledge to do very basic Internet marketing.

The John 3:16 Marketing Network is not designed to do the hard work of marketing your book for you. Those who have enjoyed the network the most and achieved best-seller status have made the most of the Internet for promoting their book. We have around two hundred fifty authors now, and even if only one-fifth of the authors help on a launch, we are reaching huge numbers of potential buyers. As we grow, I look forward to reaching a million people on launches and boosting rankings even higher in subcategories. I also encourage authors to use sources outside the network to launch a book, increasing his exposure.

Question: Does everybody who submits his or her name to join the John 3:16 Marketing Network get accepted into the network?

Answer: Even assuming a person meets all the criteria as listed on the submission page, no. As time has passed, I have become more selective. For instance, early on, if someone didn't leave all his information, which is basically, his name, website/blog, and email, if I had his email, I would follow up in an email and ask him for his full name or blog.

I don't do that anymore. If an applicant can't follow the directions on how to apply, I would rather he not join. The rules are specific about how to launch a book to best-seller status, and if an author can't follow the rules about how to join, he won't be able to follow the rules for hosting a launch.

Before I approve a person's admittance to the John 3:16 Marketing Network, I visit his website or blog. If I see something that raises a concern, I don't go any further in the application process. I also only let in about three or four authors per week. It is very time consuming because there are several steps in the process. I only have a limited amount of time each week to devote to new members.

Question: What is the John 3:16 Marketing Network like on a day-to-day basis?

We have a Facebook page to announce books on launch day and as publicity for the network. People find us there and become a fan, but that does not make a person a member of the network. The Facebook page is only a tiny fragment of the big picture.

We have a blog for launching books. We feature writing and marketing articles as well as a "spotlight author" day on Friday to highlight authors; a resource page for professional editors and marketing services offered by authors within the network and outside the network; and an application page for receiving new members (The links to these sites are on the last page of this book).

The most important part of the network is our Yahoo Forum, which is by invite only. You can't be a member of the forum unless you belong to the John 3:16 Marketing Network. We have a very verbose group on the forum. It is not unusual to have between fifty and one hundred email postings each day.

Question: What is my role (Lorilyn Roberts) in the John 3:16 Marketing Network?

I admit everybody into the network. I verify all the launch dates and launches to make sure each author is ready/prepared to launch and is not in conflict with anyone else's launch. I provide all the information explaining how to host a professional launch. I answer individual emails from members and oversee the general running of the network. It is a labor of love.

I had no idea when I began the network that it would be so successful. I have touched a felt-need in the Christian arena of authors and marketing. We have a connectedness and sharing among like-minded individuals. We make no distinction between self-published, POD published, or traditionally published authors. It doesn't come up in conversation on the forum, as I have seen on other forums.

A camaraderie and feeling of goodwill permeates the network, perhaps akin to what existed in the early church. We truly have something special here.

As with any group, however, it is not for everyone. You must have at least some familiarity with how to post on Facebook, Twitter, blogs, et cetera, or be willing to learn without complaining. You must be willing to follow the instructions on how to launch a best-selling and be willing to be edified—we want everyone to succeed.

As far as I know, we have done something unique—united Christian authors from all over the world in one network representing all methods of publishing. On book launches, we cheer each other on through announcements of various kinds, helping each author to achieve that coveted best-seller mark—not to boast in ourselves, but because our book will be promoted by Amazon as a top one hundred book with a Christian worldview. We share our thoughts, insights, knowledge, blogs, successes, prayer requests, and dreams. What started out as a way for authors to launch books has become so much more. I am not sure where God will take it, but, as I love to say, the best is yet to come.

Chapter Six
Are There Secret Formulas or Short Cuts for Making the Best-Seller List on Amazon?
? + ? = ?

If I knew of a secret formula, I would be a millionaire—and so would you. Secrets promising success don't remain secrets for long.

There is one sure road to the best-seller list, provided you have a good book, and that is hard work and networking. I don't know of any other way to do it. What I have discovered, however, is many authors spend a lot of time and money in less productive ways, thus coming away feeling discouraged and defeated.

Examples of comments I have heard include: "I can't get anyone to review my book," "my sales are non-existent," "I don't know where to begin," "I spent money doing 'this thing' and got no results."

You also have heard this if you have been marketing for a while. I could tell some fabulous tales of "drain holes" I thought would work and didn't.

I kept the cost for joining free for the first two years, but recently have begun charging a $40 membership fee. It was either that or keeping the membership closed. As we have grown, the amount of my personal time involved has leapfrogged, but even with this one-time charge, what you receive is far worth it.

I didn't start the John 3:16 Marketing Network to become a marketing guru or use it as a source of income. God gave me the vision, but He gave me the passion to write. Without a way to promote my writing, however, I knew nobody would read my books because nobody would know they existed.

I will share a short story about my first book, *The Donkey and the King*, that I published using a Print on Demand publishing company. When my book arrived, I was ecstatic. I could at last say I was an "author."

Who could I share my excitement with? I didn't know any other authors and I did nothing to market it. I made no announcement and told nobody about my new book, except my closest friends and family. I did nothing to promote it, not even with people in my church. ZILCH! NADA!

Are you wondering how many copies I sold—maybe ten copies. Yep, I probably made the Guinness Book of World Records for the "worst-selling" book that year. Why didn't I do something to promote it? First, I didn't know how; and second, I was too shy to talk about my own book.

A couple of years later, I went on Amazon to see if *The Donkey and the King* was listed since I had never checked. Sure enough, it was there. I had one review by someone I didn't know with a rating of five stars. That was the first time it occurred to me that somebody out there might like to read my book besides my closest friends and family.

I have gone from that day to this—because God put it on my heart to start the John 3:16 Marketing Network.

The John 3:16 Marketing Network is based on John 3:16 from the New Testament in the Bible: "For God so love the world that He gave His only begotten Son, so that whosoever believeth in Him should not perish but have everlasting life."

To become a member of the John 3:16 Marketing Network requires only two things: You must believe in John 3:16 and host a blog or website.

Before we are authors, we are people uniquely gifted and loved by God. Once we look beyond what someone does and see him as we see ourselves—a human being with needs, wants, struggles, hopes, and dreams, we can relate to him better and discover things we have in common.

That brings me back to the question and the title of this piece, *Are There Secret Formulas or Short Cuts for Making the Best-Seller List on Amazon?*

The short answer is no, there are no secret formulas, but yes, there are shortcuts to make marketing easier. I will share some of my thoughts and what we do in the John 3:16 Marketing Network to help Christian authors not only launch their books but continue marketing their books over the long haul. Not everyone who joins chooses to have a formal book launch. We have "discovered" other methods to achieve best-seller status through a backdoor—more on that later.

Chapter Seven
What it Takes to Have a Winning Team

Everyone knows who Lebron James is—at least they should know. Many consider him the best basketball player currently playing the game. He can do it all—shoot from the perimeter, make free throws from the foul line, dunk the ball with great charisma, pass it through arms and legs, muscle his way through guards, and practically defy the laws of probability on a good night.

He didn't just start doing that. He's been doing it since he was young. In fact, he entered the NBA at eighteen, right out of high school, bypassing a college career.

I remember the naysayers—he's not good enough, he's not old enough, he doesn't have enough experience, in the NBA he will have lots more competition, he's not that good. I remember all those comments because I wrote them. I do closed-captioning for television, and commentators love to beat up on famous people. Actually, maybe it's not so much beating up on people, but I cringe at times when I hear what ruthless so-called experts say, thinking how I would feel if they said that about me.

Marketing is really a game. It's a big game made up of players, managers, owners, referees, commentators, and the "crowds" that watch, whether it's in a stadium, in the galley, in the stands, or in a gymnasium. Somewhere everybody fits. Those that don't enjoy sports, well, I guess you just miss the game.

Let's pretend you are a sports fan even if you aren't. I will use Lebron James as an example because he is a marvelously successful basketball player. He has done it all—except one thing that he wants more than anything else. He wants to win an NBA championship.

Why hasn't he done that yet? (When I originally wrote this piece, he hadn't. Of course, now he has, but the point is even more apropos today). After all, he's been a professional basketball player now for years. Were all the naysayers right?

Even the best basketball player in the world can't win a championship all on his own shoulders. When Lebron James was with the Cleveland Cavaliers, he tried. He did everything in his power to make it happen. He came close, but in the end, he failed.

As I am writing this, the Miami Heat is playing the Chicago Bulls for a bid at the championship. I don't know who will win. I am pulling for Miami for Lebron's sake, even though I really like Joakim Noah for the Bulls—he showed up at my daughter's nine-year-old birthday party and surprised us all.

Games are not meant to be solitary sports (except for a few like tennis). To win, it takes cooperation, commitment, hard work, perseverance, and team participation by everyone.

I have captioned hundreds of games in various sports, and afterwards, the reporter usually interviews the most valuable player and the coach. He will also interview the losing coach and one of the best-losing players if time permits. It's always interesting to hear what each coach says, and I especially love to hear the players' thoughts.

After the game, all the reporters from the various sports news agencies will gather in a pressroom and the star players and coaches will sit at a long table. The press conference often includes a bunch of "stupid" questions. Usually with grace, the players and coaches will endure the battery, probably remembering that paycheck (in the pros), and those in college get a taste of the limelight.

For those teams that are successful, it goes so much deeper than that final winning shot. It goes back to hours of practice and sacrifice; learning to play together as a team, the quirks of fellow teammates, what makes them tick and what ticks them off; and encouraging each other on how to make the other person's game better. It's about "dying to self" and embracing the concept deep down that it's not "all about me." And sometimes you have those phenomenal athletes like Tim Tebow who openly give the glory to God for his success.

How does this tie into the John 3:16 Marketing Network? Each author who has joined the network will admit to the dream of wanting to be a best-selling author. In the John 3:16 Marketing Network, this is achievable for an unknown author in subcategories. It has happened on Amazon many times in the last two years.

However, I want to remind the reader that the ultimate goal of the network is to bring glory to God through promoting a Christian worldview. If we remember the ultimate goal is to glorify God, we can have a "winning team."

That means we rejoice when someone wins an award, snags a contract, receives a glowing review, or achieves something for the first time he or she never thought possible. We die to our self, not wishing it were "me" instead. God has a path for each of us. As a body of authors, we can help each other to achieve success on whatever path God sets before us. For some, that might mean selling only a few dozen books. For others, that might mean selling thousands. The outcome is not ours to control. We unselfishly commit our way to being part of a winning team, not counting the costs in personal sacrifice, but the ultimate cost of winning souls. That's the real game in Christian marketing.

It's not always the outcome that matters, but the process through which we achieve it. If we focus on the outcome and disregard relationships as we strive for that elusive finish line, we probably won't succeed. It's just too hard. Winners have learned they need others' help to succeed. This is the philosophy behind the John 3:16 Network.

Recently, an author commented to me, "I feel like I have given out so much and gotten so little in return." She cited some examples from her personal life and I could relate to her sentiments of feeling slighted. We have all experienced it. None of us is immune because it's not in our nature to ignore the hurtful things people do to us—even when it's unintentional.

My email back to her was this: *God will return tenfold what you give out if you don't keep score. He doesn't forget. Think about all the people who have helped you and you weren't in a position to return the favor.*

Believe me, you will receive it back in miraculous ways, and it's always better than what you expected, perhaps from a different source. ***But you need to have a short memory to allow God to have a long one.***

The John 3:16 Marketing Network is about a lot more than selling books. It's about being a winner—dying to self, caring about others, and encouraging each other in the journey. With the right attitude and the gifts God has given us, I have no doubt that many in the John 3:16 Marketing Network will achieve great success. There are also other kinds of success not measured in dollars and cents—in relationships, networking, gaining knowledge, and skills.

I don't want to walk away from the marketing game because it's too hard. I don't want to sit in the stands watching others sell their books while I languish because I don't know how. I don't want to be stuck on the bench because I am injured—whether it's my hurt feelings or pride that has tainted my attitude and made me selfish. And I don't want to be a commentator finding fault with everything someone else has done wrong. I don't want to be a referee—I just want to play. And those commentators out there—I can hear it from the naysayers—they probably think I am a little crazy. Well, guess what? My kids would probably agree with you (but they love me anyway).

Here we are all winners. We have taken that first step in successful marketing—networking. Prayerfully consider what you can offer to others.

Chapter Eight
Roaches That Eat Your Best-Seller Dreams

Many years ago my ex-husband and I drove to Gainesville, Florida, from Augusta, Georgia, when he was finishing medical school and applying to residency programs. We had brought along our dog, Shelley, and it was dusk after the long eight-hour drive before we arrived at the motel.

As I headed into the bathroom exhausted, I was aghast to discover the ugliest creepy crawler I had ever seen—a huge, brown roach with antlers (okay, they were feelers, but they looked like antlers), crawling around on spiny, hairy legs, and the worst part—he turned his head and stared at me with dark beady eyes.

I ran out of the hotel room screaming at my husband, "I saw a roach." After calming me down, we went back in so he could murder the invader, but the roach had scampered away. Of course, I insisted that we find him. As we examined the room in minute detail, we started seeing roaches everywhere—on the walls, on the floor, in the bathroom, crawling on the bed—I stood there and cried, "I can't stay here."

It was a football weekend, and if you know anything about Florida Gator football, you know that means almost every motel is full. We went from motel to motel for hours after driving all day to find one that had a vacancy that would accept dogs.

While my husband was contemplating an important interview for his residency, I was facing the horror of sleeping in a roach-infested hotel room. It was many years after that experience before I could stay in a hotel and not do the standard "roach check" – inside the bed sheets, under the bed, the dark bathroom, the closet—I would turn out the lights after I got into bed and then five minutes later turn them back on again to make sure one hadn't come out of hiding.

As I learned later, because my husband did accept that position at the University of Florida, there are many species of roaches besides those big ones. There are little ones, ones that fly, ones that hide in dark places, and ones that fall into the water while you take a bath (I would know).

What does a roach-infested hotel have to do with book marketing? When my husband finished medical school, I had huge hopes and dreams. I had spent the first five years of our marriage supporting him while he was in medical school in a job that was less than satisfying. I couldn't wait to take the next step towards my dream of earning that elusive college degree, which didn't include meeting a roach upon arrival.

The roaches of life have a way of catching us off-guard. They appear out of nowhere when we least expect them, and usually at the worst opportune time. Recently I had my one-another group over for prayer and put out a nice spread of food. While enjoying the sweet fellowship of Christian believers, one of my guests pointed out a large handsome roach crawling across the floor towards the table of food. That pang of embarrassment at an unexpected moment, we have all been there. I ran and fetched the roach spray. Such is life in Florida for those folks who live in Canada and the hinterlands.

As authors, we hope that story we have been mulling around in our heads becomes the next bestseller, but what about those marketing roaches? Have you met one? They are those "horrid things" that threaten to make an even bigger mess out of your best-seller dreams. They rob you of sleep, steal your money, destroy relationships, and take away your peace of mind, filling you with worry, apprehension, and doubt.

I encountered my first roach in marketing when I went to a writer's conference in the Southeast. "No one reads memoirs" several people commented. Many attendees ignored me when they realized I wasn't a VIP—an editor, agent, or well-known author. Others sounded judgmental with comments like, "Did anyone edit your book?"

I came home and wanted to crawl back into my little cubbyhole and forget all about marketing. The experience squelched my creativity and motivation in one fell swoop. Even the proposal that I spent several days working on that an agent asked me to send him following the conference was ignored.

I've learned there are a lot of roaches in the publishing business, and I have by no means met them all. On the forum, some of my fellow authors have shared some of their experiences with other kinds of roaches that I didn't even know existed.

My first step to a healthier mindset was to quit focusing on all the things I couldn't do or control and figure out what I could do. I found I could do a lot more than I thought if I just took the time to learn how and wasn't so impatient. Your roaches are probably different from mine, but whatever they are, they will handicap you more than you realize unless you deal with them. You will be able to do more than you think if you have a teachable spirit, a positive attitude, and invest some time in helping others.

When you help others, you are really helping yourself. How? I don't know how, except it's one of the laws of nature that seems to work itself into equations that have eternal value. God sees it all and rewards us in ways we least expect.

I had to go back to my faith and recommit my dreams. Nobody can do anything to prevent God's perfect will in my life if I trust in Him. No one has any power over my mental state except if I willingly relinquish that power to him. In the process of adversity and difficulties, God makes us strong. Nothing is ever wasted without serving a useful purpose.

Nevertheless, it's important to be aware of the more common kinds of roaches in marketing. A couple of months after my book was published, I bought two pricey email blast services—the kind where companies send out book announcements to their email lists, including subscribers, libraries and bookstores. Beware—these pricy roaches in the end were worthless. I sure wish I had that $600 back.

There are some other not-so-subtle roaches in marketing— laziness. If you are not willing or you don't want to work hard at marketing, I hope you have some influential contacts. You've probably heard this before but it's worth repeating: Nobody cares about your book (if they don't know you). Your job is to make people care. How do you do that? Through building relationships. I won't say any more about this now, but will address it later in "It's All About Relationships."

For those who have day jobs, kids, school, and major commitments outside of writing, I feel your pain, and this is where my concept of **"process"** comes in. **I must focus on what I can do and leave the outcome in God's hands.**

The roach of discouragement: **Quit complaining and ask God to help you**. The John 3:16 Marketing Network is all about encouraging and lifting each other up. If you are hoping that "best-seller" status will bring you happiness, it won't. There is truly nothing "out there" that will fulfill you. Only your relationship with God, family, and friends can bring you happiness.

Now that we have dealt with some major roaches in marketing, let's look at some things you can do to start marketing effectively. Before we begin a best-seller campaign, we need to look at what goes into launching a book, focusing on Amazon.

What you must do—long before you approach anyone to help you. We've had authors come into the network who did not have these things in place. Without fixing them, their book launch was doomed to failure.

Make sure your book has been edited completely—no ifs, ands, or buts. In addition to a professional editor, ask some beta readers to read your book and look for things that are wrong, unclear, or misleading—from grammatical errors to content issues to structural problems. I guarantee you, honest people will find the problems—even though your mother will tell you it's wonderful the way it is. **All the networking and promoting in the world won't salvage a poorly written book.**

Beta readers—we now have beta readers in the network to help find flaws with content. The process has not been fully implemented yet, but should be soon.

In my opinion, e-books are the wave of the future. Price e-books lower and you will sell more copies. While top-selling authors and major publishing companies can price Kindle books, for example, at nine or ten dollars, a low-profile author will be hard-pressed to sell his books at such a high price point. Remember, you must be competitive to sell books, which includes pricing your book at a competitive price with similar books by similar authors. Particularly with Kindle books, I would recommend a book be priced no more than $4.99 for a low-profile author. Even at this low price, with the 70% author royalty on

Kindle, an author can make more money on a Kindle e-book than he can on most printed books.

Unless you enroll your book in the KDP Select on Amazon, you should not only publish your book on Kindle, but in other e-formats as well. Smashwords is an excellent publisher for expanded distribution of e-books. One note of caution: Many authors have experienced difficulty removing e-books off websites, so if you want to put your book into KDP Select, don't distribute your book on Smashwords. KDP Select requires exclusivity of e-books on Amazon (more on this later).

How do you determine what are the Best Search Keywords to use when you upload your Kindle book to Kindle Direct Publishing? If you are like me, you will think about what your book is about and start with that mindset. I chose "redemption" as one of my Search Keywords for my book *The Donkey and the King*.

While it's true my book is about redemption, is a mother really going to enter that Search Keyword to look for a book for her four-year-old son? As an author, I was describing what my book was about, Christian redemption, but a parent or prospective buyer will be thinking in terms of his son or daughter – entertainment, bedtime story, Bible story, or something along those lines.

Another Search Keyword I had entered was "fantasy." While *The Donkey and the King* is a fantasy book, there are also 50,396 other fantasy books on Kindle. Before I changed my Search Keywords, my children's picture book for four to eight-year-olds had about as much chance of appearing on the first page of a fantasy search as I have of being the next President of the United States. Besides, is a father going to enter the word "fantasy" on Amazon to search for a good Christian book for his five-year-old daughter?

As you can see, I wasn't thinking like a buyer. I was thinking like an author. When you choose which Search Keywords, think as if you are a buyer –who is your audience? What do they read?

I eventually entered these Search Keywords for *The Donkey and the King*: Christian picture books, books for children, children's fantasy books, children's story books, children's Bible stories, children's classics, favorite children's books.

Note that it doesn't have to be just one word. You can enter several words as a phrase which counts a single Search Keyword.

A couple of days later, I did a search with these words to see if my book came up in searches. In "favorite children's books," *The Donkey and the King* came up as number 25 of 151 books – on the second page, which is not bad. Still, I have a bit of work to do. You along with thousands of other authors are vying for the top spots, and there can only be fifteen on the first page. This is just one peg in the broader scheme of Amazon marketing, but it's important to give detail to every step in the process. Focusing on the nuances can make a difference when it comes to the bigger picture.

Where does one go on Amazon to enter these magical Search Keywords when publishing with Kindle Direct Publishing or KDP Select? As of January 2013, to publish your e-book on Kindle, the first thing you must do is upload your manuscript to the Kindle Direct Publishing Platform at https://kdp.amazon.com/self-publishing/dashboard. If you haven't set up an account yet, you will need to do that first. Amazon will prompt you.

Assuming you have set up your account, you will be taken to the Dashboard page. At the top of the page, you will see Bookshelf, Reports, Community, and KDP Select. Below that you will see two options: Actions and Add New Title. Let's assume for this discussion, you have already added your book and you want to check and see how you entered your seven Search Keywords.

Select the desired book, choose Actions at the top, and click on the down arrow beside it. Then click on Edit Book Details. Scroll down to number three. You will see Options, Add Categories, and underneath that Search Keywords. Here is where you insert your seven Search Keywords for your book. Remember, Search Keywords can also be a phrase—not just one word.

Amazon will use these Search Keywords to help people find your book when a potential buyer enters a Search Keyword from the Amazon Home Page. I know this sounds rather elementary, but I was surprised when I snooped around Amazon looking at search phrases and then compared them with what Search Keywords I had used with my books. **The disparity between what I thought were good Search Keywords and how Amazon used them was rather embarrassing.**

With another one of my books, *Children of Dreams*, when I originally uploaded it on Amazon, the book was buried so deep in "adoption" as a Search Keyword on the Amazon Home Page I could never pull it up. I later wished I had added a Subtitle to help with search engine optimization; i.e., Two Adoption Stories In One. Less time would have passed for my book about adoption to be found in searches. Two years later, however, *Children of Dreams* is coming up on page four, number 53 out of 2,311 books. The ranking varies from day to day. I have seen *Children of Dreams* higher recently, but even if you have made mistakes along the way, all is not lost. Many other factors influence where a book appears in an Amazon Search Keyword with buyers. However, if you aren't particular about what words you put in the Search Keyword box after uploading your Kindle book, your climb out of the abyss of undiscoverability will take longer.

While entering the Best Search Keywords won't guarantee success in marketing your book overnight, you can be assured that readers will stand a better chance of finding your book out of the millions on Amazon, and small steps like this will ensure hope for giant leaps in your overall marketing endeavors.

Book Reviews

Get as many reviews of your book as possible. The new requirement before you can host a book with the John 3:16 Marketing Network is you must have ten reviews that equal a 4.2 minimum star rating. This is the absolute minimum. The more reviews you have, the better. If your book launch is on Amazon, those reviews should be on Amazon. If a prospective buyer checks out your book, you want to have some glowing reviews to encourage him to click that buy button.

Inside-the-Book Widget

Take advantage of all the functionalities of Amazon.com to market your book; i.e., the inside-the-book widget. It allows others to sample your writing before buying your book. For those who do not know what that is, if you look at most of the books on Amazon, you will see on the book cover the words, "Click to look inside." When you click on the book cover, it will open up to another screen with the first several pages showing inside the book. You can tell a lot about a book by just reading the first couple of pages.

Underneath the title of your book appears your name that is hyperlinked to your Author Page. Make sure you upload a nice photograph of yourself for your avatar on your Author Page. While I love those goofy animal shots, I am not so sure if they pass the screen test for promoting oneself as a professional.

The Author Page is set up by you through the Amazon Author Central portion of Amazon. The Author Page will show your profile, bibliography, published books, book trailers if you upload them, and a link to the Amazon Associates Program. The Amazon Associates Program will allow you to sell Amazon books on your website or blog (more on this later).

All these things can sound intimidating at first and overwhelming, but if you take your time learning, you can use these tools effortlessly. Because they are technical in nature rather than creative, all an author has to do is switch to the other side of his brain, which is where most adults spend their life anyway.

Again, I repeat, anybody can do these things. I will explain in more detail later how to access the Author Central Page on Amazon when we talk about setting up your book's categories and subcategories. Make sure you fill out all the information on your Author Page as prospective buyers will go to this page to learn more about you. I am surprised at the number of authors who haven't even uploaded a photograph. If you don't, you are missing an important opportunity to connect with buyers on a "free" high-profile, high-traffic website. I have even listed my email. Though I receive too much junk mail, I want to be found if someone wants to connect with me.

For those who are not familiar with the concept of categories on Amazon, I will briefly mention the importance of them here. Make sure you list your book correctly in the major category and subcategories on Amazon, going from the largest category to the smallest. It is more difficult to reach best-seller status in a huge category like fiction than in a subcategory like Christian Romance Fiction. The biggest roach-killer for the John 3:16 Marketing Network authors has been not optimizing the best-seller categories to enhance the probability of reaching best-seller status. I will go into this in specific detail in "The Amazon Factor."

Again, don't let the laziness roach eat at you. Persistence pays off.

Don't let the discouragement roach take away your dreams. As long as there is life in you, give it your best shot. Shoot for the moon. Even if you miss, you will land among the stars.

Because being a member of the John 3:16 Marketing Network requires you to have a blog, why not start one now? It only takes five minutes to set up one using Google's blogger and it's free. Write about what stirs you, interview other authors on your blog, review books, and post your reviews on your blog, Goodreads, Amazon, and other social networking sites.

Build up your Facebook contacts, Twitter followers, and create a Fan Page on Facebook. If all of this seems overwhelming, don't try to do it all today. Just focus on one activity.

What would I recommend? To be honest, I would focus on starting a blog and generating blog followers. Many in the John 3:16 Network will follow you for starters if you invite them to your site. After a few months, when you have become comfortable posting on your blog at least weekly and have some followers, I would work on generating an email list.

Recently, I have steered away from spending a lot of time on Facebook. Because the site has limited my outreach so much, I'm not sure how many people are seeing my posts. With 1500 followers and only a handful of people commenting, that's not very effective in the marketing arena.

Twitter posts are visible for a fleeting amount of time, perhaps at most a minute. While my outreach on Facebook and Twitter is somewhat dictated by the site, I have complete control over my blog and email list. I have gone back to working harder on what I originally started with—my blog, website and email opt-in list.

Seek out positive people to interact with on the Internet. Avoid roach people—those who are self-centered, negative, bitter, or judgmental. They will pull you down into a funk and discourage you from being productive.

Enjoy the journey. If you feel overwhelmed, pull out the roach spray. What do you need to kill? Examine what you are doing and consider what isn't working. Know yourself, your limitations, and your strengths. **Focus on process, not on outcome, and ask God to give you wisdom.** Also, remember what works for one person may not work for you. Don't be afraid to experiment and try something new. Nothing ventured, nothing gained.

Finally, don't give up. Join the John 3:16 Marketing Network and experience the blessing of sharing your marketing journey with others. Much wisdom is shared on the forum that can guide you in areas you may be unsure of.

I will cover in more detail later "The Amazon Factor" in launching a book.

Chapter Nine
What is a Book Launch Anyway? And Slowly, Please,
I am New at All of This

A few years ago at the Florida Christian Writers Conference, I took Randy Ingermanson's marketing class. If you ever have an opportunity to do so, take advantage of it because he is thorough, honest, and entertaining. Now that's not something you can say about most physicists! At the time he was working on one of his many books and made the comment that his goal was to hit number one on Amazon when it was released.

Of course, being the newbie that I was, I didn't know exactly what he meant, but it sure sounded impressive. I had no idea how one would even begin to accomplish such a feat.

I have found many authors are pretty much like me when I took that marketing class. While they may be on Facebook, they don't know how to use it very well (or even how to make a fan page). Most groan when you mention Twitter, struggle with uploading a .jpeg, don't know how to resize one (you've seen those monstrosities that take up a whole blog page), don't know how to use widgets—the first time I heard the word, I thought it was a wizard—or make a video, use an URL shortener, or follow someone's blog (where is the button), or the importance of even having followers.

Authors know how to do one thing—they know how to write. That's what they are passionate about. I would also rather write than do marketing. I would pay someone to do it—except I am too poor; but I don't want to take my baby (my book) that I gave birth to and present it to another writer's conference and have no one look at it.

When an agent and an editor told me to "Come back and see me when you have a thousand on your opt-in list (I had twenty-six at the time), my thought was, you just wait. I was challenged to do something that two people at the conference made me feel like I couldn't do. I wanted to prove them wrong.

I set about doing all the things writers do to begin marketing when they don't know what they are doing—except I had just taken Randy's marketing class, which ran for four days, and I learned A LOT.

Then reality set in. Have you ever tried to get a thousand followers on an email opt-in list? Even though it's easier now than before with the growth of Facebook and Twitter, it still takes time and effort. If you want to speak strictly about followers, however, Facebook and Twitter wouldn't be included in those numbers.

Recently I went into the hospital to have an outpatient procedure done (one of those rites of passage when you turn fifty). The pre-op stuff was a lot less fun than the actual procedure itself, but unless I did the pre-op, the doctor wouldn't have been able to see what he was looking for. It's the same with a book launch. You must do all the steps I have talked about up to this point in order to have a successful launch. Even if you don't have a formal book launch, you will still be taking positive steps in marketing your book for the long haul and developing relationships with other authors, editors, marketing experts, and potential buyers.

One of my goals with the John 3:16 Marketing Network has been to help authors with marketing challenges. I am surprised at the number of authors who join who are still using a 54K dial-up modem. An author will be at a huge disadvantage if she doesn't upgrade to something faster. I can't imagine being handicapped to that degree and being successful at marketing, though anything is possible. I would recommend a person have a cable modem or a fast connection, much faster than dial-up.

I was told when I took the class "How to Launch a Bestseller" that people would be more than willing to help. That was not true for me. Most people never responded to my emails who didn't know me personally. Think about when you post on Facebook, how many people interact with you? It's a small proportion, although admittedly, it's difficult to know if that's because Facebook is limiting the number of people who see your posts.

Getting reviews is not always easy either. Many don't know how to write a review or are too intimidated to post one on Amazon. Getting someone to read my book to do a review was hard before I started the network. Authors who like to read books and write reviews are already overcommitted, including myself. I have sent several copies of my book to people and never heard back from them. I wonder if those are the books that show up later on Amazon for a bargain price that pay no royalties.

To be honest, at times within the network, people have emailed me that it's been hard to get reviewers. Reasons are varied, but usually the reason is one of the following: The book has not been properly edited and the prospective reviewer doesn't want to give the author a poor review. The author has not contacted people in the network individually to ask—i.e., the author has not made an effort to develop relationships with others in the network, and relationship building is key. Remember what I said earlier, it's all about networking in this business when it comes to marketing. A third reason may be it's a topic that's narrow and not of interest to others.

In the end, those who have good books that are well-written and who make an effort to converse with others on the forum do find people to review their books, and there are people within the network who have review services that members of the network can tap into. The network has been helpful in this area, but to expect it to be the sole source of book reviews is unrealistic.

While the John 3:16 Marketing Network has become many things to many people, the network was originally founded to meet one need: Launching new books. I envisioned authors who were willing to come together and help each other, who understood the process and cared about others in the network. There were too many authors like me with good books waiting to be read and no way to market them. Despite human limitations, God is at work. We have helped many authors on many levels. We've had a positive impact in book marketing and publishing, pushing Christian books higher in sales to best-seller status in a variety of ways, and impacting what kids and adults read with a Christian worldview.

That leads to the question: What is a book launch?

A book launch is an event where you tell everybody in your little world (or big world) about your incredible, awesome, one-of-a-kind book, and then you get all of those people to tell everybody in their little world (or big world) about your incredible, awesome, one-of-a-kind book—and, as a result of the amazing world of mass media, everybody will hear about your book.

The other key factor is all the sales must go to one specific location; i.e., Amazon. The book sales over that period will surge, enabling you to hit best-seller status in one or more subcategories.

We have over two hundred fifty authors as of this writing in the John 3:16 Marketing Network. Some are beginners and some are pros, but we are all Christians. We are individuals blessed with the passion for writing. We help each other with book launches, blog postings, book reviews, following each other on social networking sites, and on and on.

I am reminded of Hebrews 12:1 from the New Testament in the Bible: "Therefore, since we have so great a cloud of witnesses surrounding us, let us run with endurance the race that is set before us, fixing our eyes on Jesus, the author and perfecter of faith, who for the joy set before Him endured the cross, despising the shame, and has sat down at the throne of God."

One of our members, Amanda Stephan, has prepared some tutorials for the John 3:16 Marketing Network (more on this later).

We have marketing gurus who offer free advice on the forum. I guarantee you, if there is some marketing opportunity out there you have a question about—i.e., is this a good publishing company to use—someone will know. The best answer is usually from someone who has dealt with the issue before.

What is a good launch? At the John 3:16 Marketing Network, we look at rankings. If we hit best-seller status in a subcategory, we are thrilled. If our rankings get pretty low in terms of book sales, we are happy.

It's important to note. Whether you reach best-seller status or not, you are gaining exposure. If a launch is well done, you've had a lot of exposure leading up to your book launch appearing on multiple blogs. Others are tweeting, Facebooking, and sharing your book with their social networking contacts. Oftentimes, people have to hear a name many times before it starts to register, "I need to watch that movie," or "I need to buy that book." We tell our authors not to get discouraged if they don't sell as many books as they had hoped. Remember, it's all about process, not outcome.

Recently, the challenge has become even greater to achieve a fabulously successful book launch. I believe several factors are at play: Facebook limiting the number of posts people see and the large number of free books offered through KDP Select on Amazon. In addition, with millions now on twitter, those postings are visible for at most a minute until they disappear off a phone or computer screen.

My personal belief is that as time passes, there will be fewer free books offered. Once people have downloaded that free book on their Kindle, they won't download it again, so the free offer is not as successful on repeated offerings. People will become more particular about what books they download, and Amazon may restrict the number of days books are offered for free or the number of times books can be offered in the program.

Free offers can promote a business (we see it all the time), but if that's the only kind of marketing a company or an author does, he will have a hard time promoting the same book on multiple free offerings.

To that end, I am encouraging authors hosting a traditional book launch to tap into the free book offers by those participating in KDP Select. Even if books are in the same category (which can be a good thing), KDP Select books are competing in the "free" category and the book being launched is in the "paid" category.

This is another example where a self-published or POD author can help an author hosting a traditional book launch, and the launching author can help the author offering a free e-gift to "sell" more free books. It's a win-win for everyone, only requiring coordination and pre-planning by the launching author. He will need to find out when authors are giving away free e-books and advertise those books on his landing page (if he is doing his own individual launch not hosted by the network).

What do advertisers do before a sale? They advertise the sale. Authors need to think like a marketer—what can I do to generate interest beyond just Facebook and Twitter? How many people can I get to host me on their blog? How many books can I give away on my blog tour? Where can I post my book launch and advertise the event? Amazon and Goodreads, for example, have an event tool to advertise a book launch—and that's where readers congregate. Authors need to take advantage of those promotional tools. We live in tough economic times—it has never been harder to get people to buy books.

KDP Select has been wildly successful and I have used it, so I am not casting dispersions on the program or denigrating it in any way, but it has created fierce competition when it comes to hosting a traditional launch. This makes it more important that an author launching his book come up with creative incentives to encourage people to "buy" his or her book. The method is tried and proven, but it's hard to compete with "free" books when there are so many freebies out there.

However, people will always pay for quality, and in the long run, traditional book launches will be successful if done professionally, tapping into the resources available—including blog showcases for as much as two weeks before a launch, and making better use of opt-in lists, in addition to Facebook and Twitter. As I said earlier, an author needs to develop a following through his own opt-in list in addition to generating followers on Facebook and Twitter.

There are also other free offers that can be advertised, including videos, podcasts, consulting, audiobooks, and contests or drawings for free printed books. We are developing this idea fully with our new launch page at http://John316MarketingNetwork.com.

At the beginning of 2013, Joseph Young, a marketing guru in the network, and I came up with a way to simplify launches. I recently emailed an article to members explaining the reasons for the changes—and announced the results of our first John 3:16 Marketing Network sponsored book launch that took place in March 2013.

Let me pause and add one caveat for the reader. This book you are reading is updated every couple of months. As I discover new ideas and come up with innovative ways to make the network more effective, we make changes in how we do things. The end result is you get the most up-to-date book you could possibly have. One possible downside is I write about marketing in the present tense. So the organization of the book may suffer a bit; but there is nothing worse than reading an outdated marketing book that is no longer relevant in today's volatile climate. What worked a year ago doesn't work now.

With that in mind, here is an edited version of that article to explain the newest way we are launching books in the network starting in March 2013—and hopefully for a long time into the future:

Marketing a book has never been easy, but recent changes in strategies by marketing gurus have made it even more challenging for new authors to be discovered. In the two and a half years since we started, we have helped many authors to achieve best-seller status on Amazon in one or more categories. Toward the end of 2012, however, several launches failed to ignite the excitement seen in previous launches. I was grieved when I saw authors who had worked so hard not reap the rewards they sought. I wondered what we could do as a network to recapture the essence of what our network was built on—helping all authors, especially those who are new and not well known, to reach best-seller status in one or more categories on Amazon.

I am excited to announce the results of our newest launch in March of 2013. While we still need to refine the process, the possibilities for the future are bright. Book launches are not dead—we have just reinvented the wheel.

Marketing continues to evolve. Sometimes I feel like we are chasing a moving target—like one of our cats when we want to put it outside and it hides under the table or under my bed. Marketing books without spending a lot of money is elusive, but it's not impossible. We just need to think more creatively, and fortunately, I enjoy thinking about such things.

First, let me share some initial observations related to changes in marketing. With the advent of KDP Select on Amazon, free books became all the hype. Dozens of sites offering free books popped up all over the web. Soon members were asking people to help promote their free book as if they were real book launches. The end result was it diluted the effectiveness of the traditional launches.

Members became burned out because they were constantly being asked to promote somebody's book. The free chapters of books from member authors often used in the traditional launches were basically worthless. Without sounding too cynical, it reminds me of my overindulgence of my daughters at times. If I give them everything they want, sometimes they don't appreciate the sacrifice I made to give them those things. Ask them to use their own money to buy something they want, it becomes apparent what they really value. We see the same thing with government entitlement programs—after a while, you start believing you are entitled to something for nothing.

I remind myself, though, that good things are worth paying for, working for, and striving for—especially when it comes to the things of

God. Therefore, I refused to believe that book launches for paid books were worthless, or that they were doomed to fail because of all the free books that can be downloaded. I just needed to come up with a way to tweak it. I asked myself, what if there was a way to combine free books with newly-published paid books. Surely both marketing tools could help to promote each other. I wanted to offer freebies that weren't books. What could we give readers that would entice them to buy books besides just giving them more free books?

I also felt like we needed a professionally-built landing page. And what if we made it a permanent link so people would come back month after month to check out our books? We could develop our own brand of John 3:16 Author books. Visitors could bookmark the page. The schedule would be the same each month. From the first through the 16th, we would showcase three to five books, and on the 17th or 18th, we would announce the winner of the prizes using http://random.org.

Before I could be sure if this new way of launching books would work, we needed to try it. We kicked off our first launch with the new John 3:16 Marketing Network launch page in March 2013. Instead of lasting one day, we promoted the books from March 1 through March 16, with the drawing for gifts on March 18.

In the past, we promoted one official day for a book launch. The new way of promoting books for sixteen days is vastly different. Someone asked me how this worked. Here are my thoughts.

To receive any kind of recognition from Amazon (which translates into them promoting your book to their customers) your book needs a high ranking for several days. No longer is one day as a best-seller in a category sufficient for Amazon to take notice. Amazon labeled my book *Seventh Dimension – The Door* a "best-seller" after it reached number one in Christian fantasy for four straight days. We can't achieve this with a one-day launch.

I also found that people are very busy, including me. A one-day launch meant if you couldn't help out on that one day, then you couldn't help the launching author at all.

For example, I was on the air all day Saturday, the final day of the launch of *Seventh Dimension – The Door*. I couldn't do anything— barely had time to check the rankings. That's why I set up the Google-Plus Hangout at 1:00 A.M. on Friday evening. That was the only free time I had for about 72 hours besides catching a few hours' sleep. I believe it's less stressful for the author to spread out marketing events over several days, gaining traction in the process, than stressing out over getting everything done for a one-day launch.

Think about it like this: When new movies are released, they hang around for a while—not just one day. The first day and the last day are the usually the most important days of a movie's release. That's what I tried to do with our new way of launching, is to give the books some time to be found by buyers on Twitter, Facebook, Linked-In, and other networking sites. You can also catch mistakes. I don't think we've had a perfect launch yet where something didn't go awry. We fight a spiritual battle with book launches. If something isn't right, this allows time to fix it.

Recently, there have also been several "untimely events." One member's launch was ruined by Hurricane Sandy. People aren't interested in books when something major is going on in the world; and lately, there seems to always be some kind of "catastrophic" event hanging over us. Perhaps it's a sign of the last days. It could even be spiritual warfare, but that gives the author some breathing room to still have a successful launch if an unforeseen event happens. Even a personal issue can wreak havoc. If your child gets sick, you won't be able to focus on your launch, and if it's only for one day—well, then what?

It allows more time for people to hear about all the books being showcased for the month, check out the free books that will be rotated month to month, and enter whatever contest or raffle is being offered in connection with the launch. I expect this to vary each month to keep the site fresh and new. We are looking for long-term visitors to come back every month to our launch page and become fans of our John 3:16 authors.

We still have a bit of work to do on the launch page but I love Joseph Young's design and creativity, building our page from my suggestions. There are hidden pages underneath the launch page with future opportunities in the works. Stay tuned. Once everything is completely set up, Joseph Young will be the coordinator for book launches. I look forward to him taking over this part of the John 3:16 Marketing Network.

In the past, authors had to either build their own landing page or hire someone to do it for them. The cost ranged from $125 to $250, depending on what the author wanted. The launch page was only good for one day and then no longer served any useful purpose. That's a lot of money for something so fleeting.

I've also found through the years the most difficult part of a book launch for authors has been the launch page. Authors didn't always understand its purpose. Some authors didn't have the live links posted in tweets and Facebook announcements or blog posts. In other words, the links went to the landing page when they should have gone to the pre-landing page (to see the free gifts, but not be able to access them yet). Other authors have forgotten about their own landing page and sent people directly to Amazon to buy their book.

Mistakes like these are costly, and I had been thinking for a while about having a John 3:16 Marketing Network landing page for all launches. That way authors didn't have to create their own or pay someone to do it. Instead of dealing with the technical issues of the landing page or finding free e-gifts to offer, their efforts could go towards writing blog posts or other launch activities.

I also thought if we launched several books at once, the costs could be shared, and we could have bigger and more enticing gifts and prizes to offer.

March 1 through March 16, we gave my new idea a try. Matthew Horn (*Nothing Good is Free*), Joseph Young (*There is Corn in Egypt*), and myself (*Seventh Dimension – The Door*), promoted our books on the new launch page. We offered a free kindle, a $50 Amazon gift card and a $10 Starbucks card using Rafflecopter. We also featured some free e-books on the landing page that readers could download. (It was supposed to be a $25 Amazon gift card, but I inadvertently increased it to $50 on a press release and felt obliged to honor it).

How successful was the launch of our three books? My book, *Seventh Dimension – the Door*, was fabulously successful. I reached number one in Christian fantasy, number one in Christian futuristic, and number one in religious science fiction/fantasy. Overall, I hit 762 in books on Amazon. In case you are interested, that translated into selling almost 400 books.

For me to reach this on a paid book made me feel like my launch was wildly successful. My book stayed at number one in Christian fantasy for about a week. By the fourth day Amazon labeled it a "best-seller" on their site. I took a screen shot of it for "prosperity." It may never happen again.

Joseph Young's book *There is Corn in Egypt* hit the top 100 in Christian education. Matthew Horn did not reach a top 100 in any of his categories. I haven't asked Matthew how his categories are set up, but I wonder if they were narrow enough. It is easier to reach number one in a less competitive category than a broader category.

Our goal is not to hit number one in all Amazon books, though that would be a lofty achievement, but probably unattainable for any of us in the network (except for Jerry Jenkins), but we can reach number one in a narrow subcategory given the right circumstances—mainly, a lot of hard work, networking with the members of the network, connecting with readers outside the network, and some inexpensive advertising. That's assuming you have your categories narrow enough; otherwise, you may not be able to achieve even a top 100 ranking.

You have to be realistic. Reaching number one in a subcategory doesn't mean you will sell hundreds of books, but the visibility on Amazon is quite exciting, especially when they promote your book to their customers in searches or label it as a "best-seller."

There was a bit of disparity between how well my book did compared to the others. I believe that can be attributed to the fact I did things outside of the network that helped me to sell more books. While there may have been a time I would have said the network alone could help authors to reach best-seller status on Amazon, I no longer believe that to be true. But I will say without the network's help, I don't believe I could have done it. In other words, it takes several approaches to make it happen in today's competitive environment.

First, I had partners with opt-in lists who helped to support my book launch. In the past, authors would have a launch team that provided free gifts and made announcements on Facebook and Twitter. Because we've simplified things, you don't need partners to offer free gifts.

Instead, I want to encourage everyone who is an active participant in the network to send out tweets for the book launches. If you don't feel like you can support one particular book, I hope you feel like you can still support the overall launch by the network. That does not equal an endorsement —you are sharing the books with others who then have an opportunity to check them out and enter into the drawing for prizes, including a Kindle. You are also giving your followers on Facebook and Twitter an opportunity to download free e-books.

However, launching authors still need partners to send out announcements to their opt-in lists. List partners can be encouraged to promote the launch with their email followers by letting them know they can win a free kindle and other cash prizes, Authors also need launch partners to host them on their blog, write reviews, provide endorsements, or any other launch-related activities.

What did I do outside the network to promote my book? Some of the other things I did were:

I sent out a press release to hundreds of radio stations through Christian Newswire. I was looking for visibility. One newspaper in Las Vegas contacted me and asked for a printed copy of my book, which I sent them.

I had a lot of reviews, thirty-eight right now, considerably more than the other two books. Let's face it: If two books have a similar rating, would you be more inclined to buy a book with five reviews or thirty reviews? That is the real world facing authors. Reviews make a huge difference in what books readers buy. We need authors to have ten reviews as a minimum. That's double what we have required before, and in my opinion, that is still not enough. I will talk more about this later.

While I have a lot of reviews, I don't have any endorsements that would look nice on my Amazon page.

I spent $100 and bought a listing of the editors of the top one hundred newspapers in the United States. I sent my press release out to all of them. I then sent some of them a Kindle copy of my book.

This was my thought: I wanted to ensure I sold at least some books. I figured if some of the editors didn't open or accept the free Kindle book, Amazon would refund my money. If they did download *Seventh Dimension – The Door* (and hopefully read it), the cost of sending a copy to each editor was only 65 cents. It would ensure I sold some books so in the worst case scenario my launch wouldn't be a total failure. I also thought if the editor went to Amazon to check out my book during the launch, he or she would see *Seventh Dimension – The Door* selling well and be impressed enough to go ahead and download my book. I also sent a personal message to each editor that I would love to have an endorsement.

I haven't heard from any of those editors, and I haven't checked to see how many of my books were downloaded, but I figured it was a win-win. I believe in hedging my bets for the best outcome and praying hard that God blesses my efforts.

I also contacted two advertising sites and made sure my book was sent to their email lists in addition to appearing on their websites. I have found that advertising on websites yields very few sales. How did I determine this: I used bitly.com links to track which sites gave me the most clicks.

Advertising sites with huge opt-in lists that are sent out once a day yielded quite a few book sales. (If you don't know what an opt-in list is, that's where you get an email in your inbox about bargain books). One of those sites was free and the other one cost me $25. These are not expensive sites, but they are very popular. They only advertise so many books each day. I was probably a little lucky—or maybe you could say God was in control. Either way, I know I received a bump up in sales when those two emails were sent. I'm not going to say what those sites were—if you do a launch, that information will be provided.

What about Facebook? In my opinion, Facebook is almost worthless for book promotions. I only advertised on five sites a few times –the three sites I set up, the CrossReads site once, and the Word Weavers site once, which is a closed group. I spent $15 on two different occasions in two weeks for Facebook to promote my announcement to a wider audience.

I am bothered by the fact that I have 1600 followers and Facebook is only allowing about 10 of my followers to see each post. On one of the $15 Facebook advertisements, 130 people saw my promotion. In my opinion, that is not money well spent. I won't do it again.

The only time I spend on Facebook is just to answer messages that people have sent me and to post an occasional message so that my site looks active. That's just my personal experience with Facebook.

I much prefer Twitter to Facebook. Several people have mentioned they don't like sending out the same tweet over and over, as they feel like they are spamming their followers.

First, there should be at least two or three different tweets sent out, so it's not the same one every time. I think I asked for five different tweets from the other two authors who launched with me.

Twitter is also different from Facebook. For one thing, your tweet is live for about 20 seconds and then it disappears into oblivion.

Thousands of tweets go out every hour, and so what went out an hour ago will not be seen later. That's why it's good to retweet several times during the day, but you don't want to tweet the same message every time. Twitter won't allow it anyway. You need to vary them and see which ones generate the most response.

Recently at the Florida Christian Writer's Conference, several people said that an author is expected to have 5,000 followers on Twitter.

I would add to that, more important than a Twitter following is an opt-in list. You need to build your own reader base—your own fan base. In my opinion, that's the number one thing you should focus on—not Facebook and not Twitter. You need to have a blog or website and you need to build an opt-in list. Your goal should be five thousand readers who are subscribed to your opt-in list. I still have a ways to go to achieve that.

When I first started out, I built my website and my opt-in list at the same time. Then I got away from that and focused on Facebook. I regret that I didn't put more time into my opt-in list. I now see its value more than I did before. You have total control over your opt-in list, unlike websites like Facebook which make changes that may end up leaving you completely befuddled.

An example of a recent way my opt-in list helped me is I wanted more reviews. I sent out an email to my opt-in list asking for reviewers. I picked up about 15 readers to review *Seventh Dimension – The Door* and it didn't cost me a dime. For Readers' Favorite, to get five reviews, I paid $200.

It's also important to announce your launch on other sites besides Twitter and Facebook, like http://goodreads.com, http://thebookmarketingnetwork.com/, and anywhere else you have a presence. I made several event announcements and posted them everywhere I had previously been involved.

As I have said before, one of the best ways to reach potential buyers beyond your immediate sphere of influence is to enlist "partners" to send an announcement to their opt-in list. The best way to do this is to contact friends and business acquaintances individually and ask them. So yes, you still need a launch team for your book, but you don't need to build your own landing page, you don't need to ask for free gifts, and you should be able to depend on the network to send out tweets for you.

We need to make some adjustments in the requirements for a book launch. At the Florida Christian Writer's Conference, several attendees said that publishers like to see books with 100 book reviews. Most advertising sites require ten reviews with a rating of at least four. The one thing that can set your book apart from others is having a lot of good reviews of your book.

I believe the public has gotten spoiled with so many free books appearing in their inbox. To make someone want to buy your book, you've got to make your book stand out. The only way to do this is to have lots of reviews, an outstanding book cover, a book that's priced low, and a blurb promoting your book that will emotionally grab a potential buyer. You want her to think, "I need to get this book right now," and click that buy button on Amazon. It's not as easy as you might think. People will easily fork over $4 for a Starbucks latte, but a book from an unknown author with few reviews and a mediocre book cover—not so much.

The free gifts on our new launch page will be rotated every month. Eventually we'll be charging for the placement of those books, so if you want to advertise your book, you might want to do it now while it's still free.

Each month, we will launch between three and five books. This is the same number we launched each month in the past. It's just that before we launched one book each week of the month. Many participants found that draining. We would just finish one book launch when there would be another book launch the following week. There is now only one launch per month, advertised from the first to the 16th of every month. Then there is a break until the beginning of the next month.

The tweets will be provided at the beginning of the month. You can set those up ahead of time, a few each day or a few each week, depending on how much you tweet, through the final day of the launch on the 16th of each month.

Whoever tweets the most over the course of two book launches (two months) will be awarded with a free book launch. For March's book launches, Theresa Franklin tweeted 25 times, Kimberly Payne sent out 16 tweets. Sharon Lavy tweeted 252 times, and Kara Howell tweeted three times.

These are the only members of the network who reported to me how many tweets they sent. I'm sure there were others who tweeted, but Sharon is well on her way to getting a free book launch. I might also add she has around five thousand followers.

Having a lot of followers equates to an interesting fact that most people aren't aware of. I looked up the value of my Twitter account and discovered my account is worth $1,058.36. Not that I want to sell it, but the time I spend building up my Twitter following creates a value in terms of marketing.

The charge for hosting a book launch is $155 per person—what I consider to be extremely reasonable for what you receive. Joseph Young will set up your book on the launch page, and a portion of the cost will go toward a Kindle, a $25 Amazon gift card, a $10 Starbucks card, $20 for me to do the video and launch announcement, and $25 toward a free book launch recipient. The cost may be adjusted up or down, and if there are fewer authors than three, the cost would need to be divided evenly between the two authors that would equal what three authors would pay. Five would be the maximum. With five authors launching, we would probably offer a more expensive Kindle.

Again, you will need ten reviews posted on Amazon before you can sign up for a book launch. From my observations, ten positive reviews seems to be the magic number for what reputable sites require to advertise your book. Even ten reviews are probably not enough, but it is double what we've required in the past.

How can you get ten reviews? We have about 500 John 3:16 readers that we can draw upon for book reviews. If you would like to submit your book, for $20 I will include your book and pertinent information in the monthly email to our list. I will limit the number of requesting authors to five. I can't guarantee reviews, but it's a good way to test your tease. If you don't get any responses, maybe you need to tweak it some, or improve your book cover, or perhaps your book has too small a niche. Out of five hundred readers, I would expect at least three or four to be interested in reading your book. You need to be willing to offer a print copy if that's what the reader requests. It's important you appear to be a professional author even if you don't feel like one.

The $20 charge is for my time, not to pay for a review. These reviewers are readers and not authors, so if they give your book only two stars, that's the risk you take. Since it's an individual's review, he or she can post it on Amazon or anywhere on the web. Note that it's better the reviews come from individuals. Amazon no longer allows book review companies to post reviews. The author has to post them in the editorial section of his book's placement on Amazon.

Again, Joseph Young will head up the book launches and I will send out an announcement to the John 3:16 email list. I will also make a short video for the launch similar to what I did for the launch we just had. I hope this information about our new John 3:16 launches excites members about the future of the network.

I would also appreciate any feedback. If there are ways we can make the launch page better, let Joseph know. Now that we've had a trial run, I expect more participation by members.

Thanks for sticking with me until the end of this posting. Good things are coming in addition to book launches. I am setting up beta readers for authors who are serious about making their books the absolute best, and I will be offering personal coaching as time permits.

One final thought: Let us remember who we serve. It isn't about me or you or books or rankings or marketing. It is about bringing glory to our Lord and Savior, Jesus Christ. He is the Author and Finisher of our Faith. May we always put Him first in our efforts, knowing that someday we will give an accounting for what we have done with what He has given us. Enjoy the journey, knowing the outcome is in His hands.

Chapter Ten
Why Should I Join the John 3:16 Marketing Network?

I am the president of the local Word Weavers Critique Group in Gainesville, Florida, and I have encouraged my fellow members who are serious writers to join the John 3:16 Marketing Network. Many are making great strides in their writing and working towards publication.

However, most of them are not interested in joining. The main reason: "I want to concentrate on my writing."

Doing both IS hard, but it is essential for writers to begin marketing themselves long before they finish their book.

Why? Marketing is more time-consuming and all-encompassing than writing. If you start early, you will be better prepared when your book hits Amazon and/or bookstores; and if you are a serious writer, that day will come.

Don't wait. Take some time and start making those connections TODAY—start a blog, become a member of Goodreads. Don't just focus on Facebook and Twitter, which as I said earlier, have some real limitations. Make sure you establish a Linked-In account. There are helpful discussion groups on Goodreads and Linked-In that can grow your contact list.

The John 3:16 Marketing Network combines all those assets that social networking offers with many added bonuses, including:

We help you to launch your book to best-seller status on Amazon. It is within reach for a debut or low-profile author to achieve best-seller status in one or more subcategories for a twenty-four period with some old fashion hard work and the help of the John 3:16 authors.

The forum provides encouragement and camaraderie in the Spirit of Christ.

A lot of information is shared by authors in the network—what has worked, what hasn't work, pitfalls to avoid, and ways to do things better.

We have several marketing gurus in the network who often give free help/advice/resources on our forum.

Members feature other members on guest blogs. We've had interviews of authors on blog talk radio, podcasts, and other offers of various types involving social networking adventures. Creativity reigns supreme in the network.

Because we are a cohesive group, we are in a position to test-drive new marketing strategies. There is "power" in numbers.

Your publisher will be thrilled when you tell him you have a large network of authors ready to Facebook/tweet/blog/announce your book on a book launch, and you have the opportunity to be featured on multiple websites as you promote your book. It is possible to reach thousands of people in a twenty-four period.

You will make lifelong friendships as you pour your heart/dreams/hopes and life into sharing your book and participating in helping others. As part of the Body of Christ with similar giftedness, there is nothing else like it on the web—at least that I'm aware of. If there were, I would have joined it rather than starting one.

How many things in marketing cost money and give little in return? You don't risk anything but the $40 joining fee and have everything to gain.

Chapter Eleven
How Do I Launch a Best-Selling Christian Campaign?
The Amazon Factor

I will share generally how we launch a book in the John 3:16 Marketing Network and then more specifically how to have a successful launch.

You must first have a book that you want to launch. You can launch a previously published book or a brand-new one. A book launch works equally well for both.

You must decide to which website you want to direct potential buyers for your best-seller campaign. Examples would be Amazon, Barnes & Noble, or your own website. Keep in mind that the New York Times looks to Barnes & Noble and Amazon, among others, for which books they will potentially add to their best-seller list.

What is the best day to launch a book? The best day to launch a book is on a Tuesday. More emails get opened on Tuesday than any other day of the week. That would imply to me that probably more people go on Facebook, Twitter, and other social networking sites. Mondays are catch-up days for folks. By Thursday, people are behind on their emails, and on Friday, many are already thinking about the weekend. Wednesday is the second best day. You also don't want to launch a book that would conflict with a major holiday like Thanksgiving, Christmas, Labor Day, Canada Day, or the Fourth of July. If your book is genre-specific, tie it into a special event day. For instance, if you have written a romance, Valentine's Day would be a good day to launch. *Children of Dreams*, my book about adoption, was released a couple of weeks before Mother's Day.

The Event Counter Widget on the John 3:16 Marketing Network Blogspot helps everyone to know when the next launch will be. I encourage everyone to add the counter to his blog or website. That means every book that's launched within the network has the potential to be advertised on two hundred fifty websites during the days leading up to the launch. How often does anyone have his or her book advertised on that many blogs at one time? That's not even counting the announcements on e-blasts, Twitter, Facebook, and other social networks. That gives an author tons of exposure for a book launch.

After installing the Event Counter Widget on their websites, the members don't have to do anything else with it because I update the widget and the code gets fed to all the websites automatically. If you are wondering how to put the counter widget or John 3:16 widget on your website, you can take advantage of the tutorials that one of our members, Amanda Stephan, put together for the John 3:16 Marketing Network at http://www.scribd.com/doc/56120337/Widgets-in-Blogger. She also has other helpful tips and tutorials at this link on how to do such things as resize a jpeg using Paint, Beginning Twitter, More Twitter Help, and Blog Basix. Many authors don't know how to do these things and if you need help, take some time and work through her tutorials. It will save you frustration when you do a launch later.

Sally Franz, who ran a successful campaign with her book, *Scrambled Leggs: A Snarkey Tale of Hospital Hooey* advised me: "Don't forget to emphasize that to get on Amazon Bestseller, they should 'stage' 7-10 sales in one hour on the same day. I would say between ten after the hour and ten of the hour would work, and then track your rating for that next hour (usually the new ratings post at about ten after the hour)."

How to Categorize Printed Books on Amazon

For the purpose of the next discussion, I am going to address specifically how to get printed books categorized on Amazon.

There are different ways a book can be categorized. Categories are different from tags. Tags are what people reading a book do to label how they think a book should be listed. That's not the same thing as what an author needs to do to get his book categorized to reach bestseller status.

I am going to go into specific detail here because many people have missed best-seller status simply because their books were not categorized narrowly enough in the subcategories.

Most authors are familiar with the Amazon Bestseller Rank. Unfortunately, most authors will never hit the top one hundred best-seller status on Amazon. However, that doesn't mean one can't make the best-seller list in the subcategories or sub-subcategories on Amazon. It is possible for a debut author to reach best-seller status in one or more subcategories on Amazon. The problem is that many authors don't know how.

What does being on the Amazon Bestseller List mean? Most people would say it means a book reached the top one hundred in sales at a given time. To do a book launch in the John 3:16 Network, the author should track sales for a 24-hour period. Sometimes there is a slight lag, but not so much that the highest ranking won't appear during or shortly after that 24-hour period.

I encourage authors in the network to take a "screen shot" several times during the day to try to record their lowest ranking towards number one in one or more subcategories. To take a screen shot, if you are using Windows, hit control/print screen together, go to a blank Word document, and hit Control-V. Your screen shot will appear and you can save it as a Word document.

How do you get your book categorized on Amazon in subcategories? This is crucial for a debut author to have a chance to claim "best-seller" status.

Amazon has several platforms in place to help authors. One of these is their Author Central Program. If you do not have an account, the site will prompt you to set up one. The link is https://authorcentral.amazon.com/gp/home.

After entering your email and password, you will be taken to the "Welcome to Author Central" page. If you scroll down to the bottom of the page, you will see a "Contact Us" tab. If you click on this, it will take you to another page. There it will ask you to "Select an issue." You want to click on "my books." Underneath that, it will say, "select details." Choose "update information about my book." Beneath that another window will open, and you want to "browse categories." Under that another window will open, and you should choose, "I want to update my book's browse categories." There is a "Did You Know" tab and you can read more about categories, the inside-the-book program, and other important related topics.

Beneath that, you will see the number 2, and the question, "How would you like to contact us?" You can either email or phone Amazon. You will explain to them that you would like to update the categories of your book.

How do you know what categories to use? On printed editions of your book, you are allowed two categories. Don't assume Amazon will do it the way you want. It's best to be pro-active on such an important point and give them what you want exactly the way you want it.

To know what categories in which to list your book, you need to be familiar with how Amazon categorizes books. Go to http://amazon.com and look on the left-hand side for the search browser. You will notice on the left-hand side the category "department" and underneath it "books." Listed underneath books are all the main categories on Amazon beginning with "arts and photography" and ending with "travel."

You will notice that under "arts and photography" are listed 387,013 books. That means in order to reach best-seller status in this category, you will have to beat out 387,000-plus books.

Let me go down to the category "parenting & families," which has 88,692 books. If you click on that, you will see it breaks down into subcategories of adoption, aging parents, family activities, family health, family relationships, fertility, parenting, pregnancy & childbirth, reference, and special needs. *Children of Dreams* reached number eight in the subcategory of adoption, out of 1,641 paid books. That means my book has been a bestseller on Amazon in adoption books.

In the email that I sent to Amazon, I listed one of my categories as parenting & families/adoption. Since I could list two for my printed copy, I listed the second category as "parenting & families/family relationships/motherhood. The category for motherhood has 4,550 books. I also reached best-seller status in this at number eleven.

Obviously, the more books there are in a category or subcategory, the harder it's going to be to get into the top one hundred, so the narrower the subcategory, the more successful you will be.

After you have decided which two subcategories to list your book in, you will need to contact Amazon and ask them to set this up for you. Make sure you return to the previous page and you will see

Amazon gives you the option of contacting them my email or phone, as I said above. Amazon has always been prompt when responding to me, so take the time to do this. It's important to get your book categorized in subcategories, and it's less painful than it sounds.

That brings me to the second part of this discussion on categories. As I mentioned before, you must categorize your printed edition and your Kindle edition separately. With Kindle, you also get two categories. It is much easier to reach best-seller status on Kindle than with a printed book. Why? There are fewer Kindle books that you are competing against than printed books. Not every book has been published in Kindle.

According to the latest information from Amazon, here is how to get your categories set up for a Kindle e-book.

First, go to https://kdp.amazon.com/self-publishing/signin.

Second, sign into your account.

Third, click the "actions" button for the book you would like to update

Fourth, scroll down to number three, target your book to customers.

Fifth, click on add categories. That will open up to a new screen, add or change categories.

Sixth, click on the plus button in front of these main categories to open up subcategories and sub-subcategories. Make your selections.

Seven, click on save.

The screen will return to the default page, where you started. Please notice that this is also where you make other changes to your e-book, including editing your book details.

The Inside-the-Book Widget

I mentioned earlier about how important the "Inside the Book" widget is on Amazon. I believe Barnes & Noble has one also. Once again, the reason is because it allows people to sample your book. I have bought several books because I was able to flip through it (as you would do in a bookstore). If you published through Create Space, they will automatically set up your inside-the-book widget. Otherwise, you will need to go to "Author Central" again to set this up. You will see on the "Welcome to Author Central" page under "learn more," an option to join the "Search Inside the Book Program." The link is http://amzn.to/SsTMYS.

Another recently added feature available on the "Welcome to Author Central" page is the Amazon Author Rank. If you click on the hyperlink "rank" in the middle of the page, you will be taken to a page that shows your author ranking for two weeks, one month, or your all-time ranking. This is a nice feature to check and see when you ranked the highest. This is a good way to compare marketing strategies at various times versus overall sales figures.

Free e-book for John 3:16 Marketing Network Launch Partners and Book Reviews

This leads me to another important area. If you are a member of the John 3:16 Marketing Network, you need to be prepared to give a free e-book or printed edition to anyone you contact to help you launch your book. If the person you sent the book to really likes it, he might even write a review. I have done this for several people who have asked me to help them on a launch. You can read my reviews at: http://amzn.to/m9BAqX One nice thing about Amazon is they do everything they can to give an author as much exposure as possible. As a reviewer, I am ranked 10,216 with 139 helpful votes. I didn't know when I started doing a few reviews that Amazon would track my ranking on reviewing books. While that is not that high, if I wanted to spend a significant amount of time writing reviews, Amazon would reward that effort. Every little bit helps to give you exposure.

If you are an author who is new to social networking, one way to break in and make some friends is to do book reviews. Some writers' blogs focus exclusively on book reviews. You will always have customers coming to your blog site if you provide heart-felt, credible reviews for authors. You can post the reviews on Amazon as well as your blog site and ask people to follow you. Many will visit your blog to check out what kind of reviews you write and over the course of time you will build a following.

One word of caution: Don't write something that would hurt you personally if someone were to write it about your book. Many authors wear their heart on their sleeves, and in the John 3:16 Marketing Network we have some very specific rules about how to do book reviews. You will be provided that information when you join.

Recently, a reviewer on Amazon posted the following comment in reference to the above paragraph:

"In commenting on reviewing, she also says 'don't write something that would hurt you if someone were to write it about your

book' and 'in the John 3:16 Marketing Network we have some very specific rules about how to do book reviews. You will be provided that information when you join.' This, to me, is a red light that says that reviews by members of the network are not impartial, as they are effectively being asked only to write nice things about the network books they review. Such 'shill' reviews are often identified and publicised (sic) in the Amazon discussion forums, and I've lurked in enough of those discussions to know the author never wins."

I responded with the following:

"Reviews: You seem to think that we skew those in some way that is unethical. We don't, but some things must remain confidential within the network, and how we handle reviews is one of them...we don't tell authors how to rate any book. They rate them as they see fit, but I don't feel comfortable going into any more detail than that. As far as how authors obtain reviews outside the network, that's entirely up to them."

I will add my personal philosophy on book reviews. I generally won't review a book that I can't give five stars. I read lots of books for information and enjoyment, but writing reviews is work. I'm not motivated to write a review for a book that I don't like. I derive no satisfaction in cutting a book to shreds. If a book only deserves one or two stars, I wouldn't even make it past the first page. I get bored too quickly. I have refused to write reviews for books of members in the John 3:16 Marketing Network once I started reading and found "flaws." I let the author know what he needed to do to make his book better.

If you look at my reviews on Amazon, you will find fifty-three reviews. I can only remember one book I didn't give five stars. I had to review it as part of my Masters in Creative Writing; otherwise, I wouldn't have bothered. If I wrote reviews for all the books I read, my reviews would be substantially higher, but I don't want to. Many of my reviews are quite lengthy as I tend to look at writing as an art. Literary folks would call them "critical" reviews.

I want to say again, you MUST have some good reviews of your book. If you are a member of the John 3:16 Marketing Network, you need to have at least ten reviews with a rating of at least 4.2. If your book launch is on Amazon, those reviews should be on Amazon. If someone is interested in your book, you want to have some glowing reviews to encourage that person to buy your book.

I know some of this is common sense, but I have been surprised by the number of authors who have wanted to launch a book who had no reviews. If I don't know an author, I won't want to help her launch her book unless she has others who vouch for the quality of her book. I've read a lot of the books for which I have been involved in launching, but there are some kinds of books that I don't read, so I need to rely on other peoples' reviews to feel comfortable attaching my name to it, whether it is just a tweet, a Facebook announcement, or other launch-related activity.

If you go to this link— http://amzn.to/WdAhkv, you will be taken to my review page where it will list all my reviews as well as other interesting information. You will see that I have written fifty-three reviews, created two Listmania! lists, and have uploaded ten images. On the left side is my avatar and one hundred thirty-nine "helpful votes." If you are wondering how the voting happens, if you look at a review of any book (except your own), you will see underneath each review the phrase, "Was this review helpful to you?" followed by yes or no. This is where readers can vote on whether a review is helpful to them in deciding whether to purchase a book.

I will admit, if someone writes a "not so nice review," I will vote "no, this review is not helpful." I would prefer to have less glamorous reviews that are fair ranked above those that are not, so I vote against those that are not useful as a deterrent to unfair reviewers. At least my negative vote goes against their statistical ranking of helpfulness to readers.

The percentage is posted under the author's profile on his review listings page. You can see mine at the above link. I have received 140 out of 155 helpful votes on reviews for a 90 percent rating. You will also see other information on this page that I feel is helpful for connecting with readers.

Because several people in the network have asked recently what a Listmania! list is, I will explain it here. A Listmania! list is a list of books that anyone can put together that will act like a prompt—here are some books you might like based on previous books you have purchased—when someone searches for a particular book or type of book (inspirational, romance, et cetera) on Amazon. This is my inspirational Listmania! list: http://goo.gl/9yoyE. If you click on it, you will see sixteen books by different authors, my book *Children of Dreams* among them. Again, the Listmania! list lets a buyer know about similar books he might be interested in purchasing based on what he is searching for.

If you want to make your own list, go to the page where you book is located on Amazon, and you should see something similar to what is on my page. Towards the bottom of the screenshot is "create a Listmania! list." You click on that and follow the prompts. My page shows three Listmania! lists my book *Children of Dreams* appears in, two created by me and one by someone else.

I am taking the time to point out these items because all these marketing options can help you to build an Amazon platform. I prefer to host my book launches on Amazon because they do so much to help authors promote their books. I don't have to pay for the statistics or information Amazon provides, and this is just a small sample of what Amazon offers to authors.

In conclusion, I want to highlight a couple more features that are unique to Amazon of which authors should take advantage.

How to Become an Amazon Associates Affiliate

One is the Amazon Associates opportunity. For a long time I didn't consider it because it seemed overwhelming to figure out how to use it, but it's not. Basically the idea behind being an Amazon Associate is you can put new and used Amazon products—like books, music, audiobooks, even toys and sports apparel—on your blog or website and make money. You can use the products to bring people to your website which increases your rankings on Google. The link is http://bit.ly/SsUDbY.

When you go to the page, you will see on the left-hand side a phrase "get started now." You will need to set up an account by answering a few simple questions, and Amazon will check out your website or blog to make sure it is legitimate. Once they approve you, they will email you a "tracking id" code that they will be put inside the .html of the product that you post on your blog (like your book). You will go to your Amazon Associates page every time you want to post an Amazon product on your website so your "tracking id" code will be included in the .html. It's nothing harder than cutting and pasting a bunch of funny-looking combinations of letters and numbers.

When you paste a link on your site, by using the code they have provided you, it lets Amazon know that you sold this book on your website or blog. They will pay you, as an affiliate, a small amount for the item a customer bought off your site. You can also add a few fun things like widgets or a slideshow, or go all out and create an aStore. It's a great way to promote your own books as well as your favorites, and in the process, make some money. Small amounts add up.

New Feature on Amazon: KDP Select for KDP Authors & Publishers.

Any Kindle books you have published on Amazon can be entered into the KDP Select. It's the exclusivity that makes this a unique Amazon feature. You must remove your e-book from other distributors, like Smashwords and Barnes & Noble (even your own website or blog) for at least ninety days.

KDP Select titles can be advertised free for five days every ninety days. If you have U.S. rights, your Kindle book will be entered into the Kindle Owners Lending Library. Each time your e-book is loaned to another qualified member of the program, you can earn a certain percentage back, based on a complicated set of algorithms that I don't understand. I didn't give it much thought until one of our members shared recently on the forum that he had made a couple of hundred dollars the previous month based on the number of times his book had been loaned out by members.

Some authors in the network have "sold" thousands of Kindle books for free during the time their e-books have been free in the KDP Select. While they didn't receive royalties, their Kindle books were widely distributed, and many ranked in the top one hundred "free" Amazon e-books. When Amazon returned their e-books to the "paid" category, briefly they maintained their best-seller ranking, becoming a best-seller of sorts by default. In many instances, the increased sales of e-books carried over into print books or other books they had published. To learn more about KDP Select, visit: http://kdp.amazon.com/self-publishing/KDPSelect. Also see Chapter Twelve in this book.

How Many Books Have I Sold?

Finally, you are selling some books—e-books and printed books, or p-books. You want to know how many, especially after a book launch, but it takes a while to find out from your publisher. Your ranking gives you some idea, but you might also wonder where you are selling your books. A new feature on Amazon Author Central will give you the information. Again, the link to Amazon Author Central is https://authorcentral.amazon.com/gp/home. Here you can check to see how many print books you have sold (Kindle has a different website).

If you look, two-thirds the way down are the words "sales info." If you click on that, you will be taken to another screen that will open up to a map of the United States (at least where I live; it is probably different if you live in another country), showing where you have sold books. To the right it will say "geographic areas," and beneath that it will show more specifically where you have sold books.

To check and see how many Kindle books you have sold, for example, during a KDP Select Free day, you need to go to your Kindle Author Dashboard at https://kdp.amazon.com/self-publishing/dashboard and sign in. There you will see all of your e-books listed. If you click on one of the books, it will open up to another page. At the top, you will see Bookshelf, Reports, Community and KDP Select. If you click on Reports, you will be taken to your royalty page with three different options: Month-to-Date Unit Sales, Prior Six Weeks' Royalties, and Prior Months' Royalties. If you click on one of those listings, you will see a detailed listing of the books you have sold, units refunded, and units borrowed. Amazon updates this daily so it's a valuable tool to gauge how successful your various marketing strategies might be—and if you made, for example, an appearance on a television or radio show, if that helped you to sell more books.

Knowing most of the information featured in the "Amazon Factor" will be vital to a successful book launch. While some of it is not essential, all of the "factors" outlined will go a long way towards giving you not only knowledge in the short-term for a launch but also in the long-term.

A launch is a sprint—it gets you going and jumpstarts your book marketing efforts. However, you also want to market your book for the long haul. If you only focus on your launch, afterwards, your book rankings will fizzle if you don't have a long-term plan in place. In fact, without a long-term plan, even with a successful book launch, you will not sell as many books as you might have hoped. So before I get to the final section on launching a book, let me mention a marketing book I would highly recommend, written for debut and low-profile authors—authors who aren't famous—to help you maximize your marketing efforts following your launch. It is *Sell More Books,* by J. Steve Miller and Cherie K. Miller. They give practical advice that will help you to continue to market your book during the weeks following your launch. I read some early drafts before it was published and found a lot of helpful information.

To finish up on how to launch a successful Christian book through the John 3:16 Marketing Network, there is one more important platform that you must give considerable attention to—**social networking**.

Internet social networking adds a feature to launching a new book that formerly was unheard of. It has changed the landscaping of marketing, which is especially appealing for an unknown author with few publishing credits. Authors have unprecedented access to a vast network of community, including authors, editors, publishers, the reading public, and everyone in-between on a host of websites. The two most common social networking websites are Twitter and Facebook. If you decide to go the traditional route to publishing, editors and agents will expect you to have a thousand followers on Facebook and Twitter.

While these sites and others offer more to authors than existed in the past as far as connectedness, they didn't provide what I wanted to be able to do on a book launch. I wanted a network of like-minded Christian authors who understood what was involved in launching a book and would be willing to help me (and one another). I cover the background of this in the beginning of this book extensively, so I won't repeat it here.

It has been two years since I went ahead with my idea. I've been blessed to see how God has brought two hundred fifty plus authors together in the John 3:16 Marketing Network. What started as a dream is now a reality. We share not only book launches but many other aspects of marketing as well. In addition, as Christians, we lift each other up in prayer and encourage each other personally and professionally.

We've had many book launches in the John 3:16 Marketing Network in the last two years and it's been an ever-evolving learning experience. I have found certain key components are like a "formula." Those who follow it achieve greater success in reaching best-seller status than those who don't.

Now, let's get to the nitty-gritty and see what enables many relatively unknown authors to reach the coveted "best-seller" status in subcategories on Amazon.

Chapter Twelve
It's All About Relationships

The secret to getting people excited about your book is through building relationships. As you share your own passion about your book, you will ignite others to share in your excitement. The "others" who buy your book, if they like it, will share it with their "others." Every bestseller that has ever been written began with the author, who shared it with another person, who shared it with another person, and on and on.

If it's that simple, then why is it so hard to sell a lot of books? Part of it is that you are competing against, on Amazon alone, over seven million print books. **Most people won't spend their hard-earned money to buy a book from an author they don't know unless it's on a topic they are interested in or a book that comes recommended.**

One way to be unsuccessful, especially in today's over-saturated marketing and advertising world, is to become too self-absorbed and forget that people who don't know you won't care about your book. If you approach someone focusing only on your own need, "help me with my book," the other person is probably going to think, "What's in it for me?"

When I took a class on "How to Become a Bestseller," one of the comments that was repeatedly made was people will want to help you sell your book. I can say that was not my experience. In the beginning, when I contacted people cold turkey (before the network was in existence), whom I didn't know, 99 percent of them never responded. Of the one percent who did, the answer was no.

People are busy. Unless a person knows you, the reality is, he won't care about your book. How do you make people care? You care about them. As Christians, if we use Jesus as our example, who would have listened to Him if He hadn't cared about the people around Him. Jesus loved everyone unconditionally and ministered to their needs abundantly.

Lest you think I am saying we need to be like Jesus to that extreme, the reality is, that won't happen. But if we put that picture in our head and use it to guide us, we will approach people with a different mindset. We won't want to use people for our own ends and treat them as if the only value they have is to help us sell our book. We can build a deeper relationship that will have greater value. If you are in this for the long haul, those relationships will be a lot more meaningful than the one book you sold out of the two hundred thousand people you spammed on an email blast that cost $200. Meaningful relationships are free, or should be. The question is not what someone else can do for you, but what can you do for him?

Back when I tried unsuccessfully to put together a best-seller campaign and couldn't find anyone to help me, I prayed about what I was doing wrong. I was told in the Best-Seller class that people would want to help me, but that wasn't true. Why? I had not built those kinds of relationships in the publishing world; and the writers' conferences I went to offered little encouragement. In fact, at certain points, they were dreadfully depressing.

What was wrong with this picture? I asked God to show me what to do because I was frustrated. When I asked, God showed me: Build a network of Christian authors to launch books. The name and idea was instantaneous—I knew God was giving me a vision.

Two years later, even within the John 3:16 Marketing Network, the same scenario applies. Those who invest in getting to know the other members of the network at a deeper level have more supporters for their launch and sell more books. It's just a law of logic that if you have fifty partners on your book launch, you will probably have more exposure than if you only have ten.

Contact Authors Individually to Help You Launch Your Book

You need to consider who you want to contact. If you write a mystery, you will probably have more success getting people who like mysteries to help you than contacting those who are nonfiction devotional writers.

In the John 3:16 Network, I encourage an author launching a book to visit the blog or website of the person he wants to ask. Be interested in the other person and find out what kind of author or blogger he is.

Do you have any hobbies in common, kids of a similar age, live near one another? When you start digging around in people's websites, you might be surprised at what you find. I remember visiting the website of a prospective author for the network who lived in New York who had been on the same television program I was on in Atlanta, and I live in Florida. It's little things like this that help you make a connection with someone. Once you connect with someone, it's easier to ask for help. At the very least, the person you ask shouldn't feel like he is being used.

Human nature is to take the path of least resistance. It's easier to send out a blanket email to a group of people at once, "please help me with my book launch." In some ways it's less intimidating. If someone doesn't want to help you, he can ignore you more easily. Many of us fear relationships. We don't want to get hurt, but as it is in life, if you don't risk anything, you won't accomplish anything.

The last thing I want members doing is spamming other members with "please help me" several times throughout a launch. The rule in the network is that you can send out one general announcement of an upcoming launch, ask if anybody wants to help, and some will reply. After that, you must contact members individually.

You can send out a group notice shortly before your launch, reminding the network about your launch and encouraging those who are not launch partners that they can still help by sending out Facebook and Twitter announcements on your "big day."

Include several Facebook announcements and tweets in your post that people can cut and paste. Many will pre-post their tweets in advance so the book launch promotions will go out at various intervals throughout your launch day.

Oftentimes the day of the launch, members will check the rankings and announce if someone has gotten to best-seller status in a category or subcategory. It can be very exciting.

Early on, it was difficult for members to contact each other because they had to contact members through their websites. We came up with the Yahoo forum, and that not only made it easier but provided a wonderful opportunity for members to connect on a daily, even hourly, basis. The network is quite verbose. I will make another comment on this later.

Now you know the secret of how to have a successful book launch: All the nitty-gritty of Amazon; you know the proper way to do it—through personal emails and contacting people one-on-one; if you have joined the John 3:16 Marketing Network, you have the benefit of many critique pieces written by authors who have had previous launches uploaded to the forum that you can peruse, and you have a network of Christian authors to help you.

You might wonder, what is the best way to contact people in the John 3:16 Marketing Network?

You can contact other authors directly on the Yahoo forum at http://groups.yahoo.com/group/John316MarketingNetwork/. If you are not a member you will not be able to post. It's a closed group requiring membership in the John 3:16 Marketing Network. If you decide to submit an application or are already a member, please bookmark the following link in your favorites for future reference: http://groups.yahoo.com/group/John316MarketingNetwork/

For those who are a little less verbose, the settings can be adjusted to receive messages once a day, special notices only, or no emails. The above link will take you to the members' page. Click on the "members" link, which will take you to the members' part of the forum. Click on the beginning letter of your email address, and it will take you to the page where your information is listed. This is where you adjust how you want to receive your emails: On the right-hand side you will see your email. Underneath your email, there is a box to adjust how you want to receive your emails. The choices are: individual emails, daily digest, special notices, or no email.

Special notices will only come from me and are important messages pertaining to the workings of the network. Set your preference here for how you would like to receive your emails. Do not unsubscribe from the forum unless you no longer want to be part of the network. Depending on how busy I am at the time, I may or may not contact you before removing you.

You can also view other members' email on this part of the forum and can contact members individually through a "send message" or by personal email. This is best way to contact other members when you are hosting a book launch.

Mine is set to receive individual emails. Again, this is where you change the settings to meet your needs. **Please do not unsubscribe from the forum if you only want to reduce the number of emails you receive. You will be booted off.** Some members thought that's how they changed the settings (they didn't want to receive so many emails), and I had to put them back on again. Hopefully this will clarify the correct way to adjust the number of emails you receive. If I sound redundant, it's because I need to be to make sure everyone understands.

The members section is an important part of the network, but there are also other locations on the forum to tell people about your books. You can also list your web/blog information so authors in the network can get in touch with you for book launches or other marketing opportunities.

We have an important files page where documents have been uploaded that pertain to book launches—what authors have learned that they are willing to share with others.

We have a data base link on the forum that until recently has only been used by a few authors. It is found on the left-hand side of the home screen, down a few notches under "links." If you click on "data base," you will be taken to a table. Here a member can enter his name, email, address, city, state, zip, website, campaign site, and blog. If members enter all their information here, it will make it easier for authors on book launches to have all the pertinent details in one spot for contacting members. Of course, this is not mandatory, but it would be helpful.

The idea of the John 3:16 Marketing Network initially was to enable authors to have partners to help launch their books; authors who have done it know how hard it is to put together a campaign, and often they will be the most helpful to a new author .

Because my goal from the beginning has been for members to develop relationships with each other, the network has become more than just a vehicle to launch books. There is a feeling of camaraderie and caring. I have been blessed immensely by the friends I have met, and what was once an insurmountable task—finding people to help me—has now become an unbelievable blessing. The network is continuing to evolve. Other ways to interact and share have developed, including book reviews, blog tours, blog hosting, author interviews, and connecting on Facebook and Twitter.

We have also produced our first book, *Taste and See, A Sampling of First Chapters by John 3:16 Marketing Network Authors*. We had sixty authors who contributed the first chapter of one of their books or offered other writings as a promotional tool for the network. Hopefully readers will find this an innovative way to discover new authors.

Now that you have personally contacted a significant portion of the members in the John 3:16 Marketing Network to help you launch your book (and don't forget to contact people outside the network that you know), hopefully you have at least fifty, maybe even one hundred people or more to announce your book on your launch date. If you have done this, and have all your Amazon factors in place, you are well on your way.

You want to make everything as easy as possible for your launch partners. Whether it's an announcement for a blog, a review, an interview, a book synopsis, Facebook blurb, Twitter post, or ezine promotion that might go out to dozens or thousands on an opt-in list, give your partners who have offered to help you all the information they need. exactly the way you want it, so that all anyone has to do is cut and paste.

If you have a picture of your book or yourself, size it down so your launch partner doesn't have an eight-by-ten photograph of your smiling face on his blog. If you can provide the .html for your announcement on his blog, the formatting will be done for him and he can just cut and paste without resizing any pictures or photographs. Some people also don't know how to do this and it would create more frustration on your launching partner's part—something you want to avoid.

For New Members

We have a couple of rules in place for new members to the John 3:16 Marketing Network, to ensure they know how to do a launch:

In addition to helping on at least two launches before a new member hosts his own, he must be a member of the network for forty-five days before setting a date for a launch. This will allow time for a new member to see how the network works, get to know some of the wonderful folks here, and make sure he has adequate time to prepare and put everything in place.

How Long Should I Prepare for my Launch

The Best-Seller Program I took recommends anywhere from one month to three months to prepare for a successful launch, and that's after several hours of training. If you cannot give at least twenty hours to a launch, you should wait until you can. For those who have been members for a while, do not feel like you must participate in every launch. Pick and choose those you feel comfortable supporting when you are contacted.

If you are contacted to participate in a launch, please respond to the author contacting you. Let him know if you can help; if you can't, be sure and let him know that, too. We have seasons in our lives when it's easier to do certain things. You will have other opportunities to help someone else. In the end, if everyone does his or her part, all will be blessed. It reminds me of geese as they fly South for the winter. When the leader of the "V" formation gets tired, he glides to the back and lets someone else lead. So it is with the network. When we all help out at different times, we contribute our varied talents and gifts, and in the end, we are all blessed.

The goal of the John 3:16 Marketing Network is to let the world know about your book and raise the public profile of books with a Christian worldview. Without exposure, no one will know your book exists. It's all about social networking in today's marketing world. Ultimately, the aim for the author is to sell books (more on this below). My goal is to promote as many Christian books as possible to best-seller status so that the reading public will have great books to read with a Christian worldview. Books that hit best-seller status garner the attention of Amazon that will highlight these books in prominent places. After all, they want to sell more books, too. Maybe someday we can get a book on the New York Times Best-Seller List.

When I began the John 3:16 Marketing Network in the summer of 2010, this quote came to mind from **Zechariah 4:10:** "For who has despised the day of small things."

It was in reference to the meager beginning of the rebuilding of the temple. While we have accomplished much in the past two years, we are still a small network. This quote resonates in my heart—God will do great things if we commit our way to Him. I pray that we can encourage and lift up each other in the network as brothers and sisters in Christ. We have much to be thankful for, and yet our needs are great. God knows even the number of hairs on our head. He has given us a diverse group of talented, Christian authors who have taught me a lot more than I ever thought I needed to learn.

Recently one of our members, Eddie Snipes, asked this question of members of the John 3:16 Marketing Network: **How do Christians write without falling to selfish ambition?**

I was struck by this profound response from another one of our members, Janet Perez Eckles:

Hi, Dear Friends,

Asking your forgiveness in advance, I'd love to give you a tad more than my two cents regarding Eddie's insight, so true and alive in us. It just so happens that I address this in my writing. These are three brief excerpts from chapter five of my book, *Simply Salsa* (Judson Press, August, 2011).

"Do you remember when an outrageously wealthy man was asked how much more money he planned to have?" He answered, "A little bit more."

How insane, I thought. He has enough cash to buy New York, and he wants more? But really, Amiga, we're all in that mode. We want just one more thing. And with new resolve and mucho passion, we set off to reach higher heights.

I confess. Here's my ambitious side exposed for all to see. Moving beyond complacency, I decided to write. And as I began, I dreamed of success. And in the process, something happened, and a bit subtly, I coveted other writers' achievements. I hoped and wished for what they possessed: Tons of literary awards and pages filled with Google links to their accomplishments. Dressed in envy green, I coveted that kind of success, imagining my book title and name on the best-selling list. And grinning with anticipation, I planned to embark on book-signing tours from sea to shining sea. My publicist would have to choose which interview request to accept first—Oprah or Buenos Buenos Dias America, and when the fat royalty checks poured in, I'd pay off our credit cards, and hubby and I would take off for a week in Hawaii.

What's wrong with that dream? That's the American way—to shoot for the stars. If we don't land on a star, maybe we'll reach the moon. The problem is we set our goals ignoring the "EV" factor— eternal value—the one that holds worth for eternity. Without it, when we reach the moon, we find it's hard to breathe, and disappointment is as big as those moon craters all around us.

Remember that blonde movie star who was famous in the 1950s? She possessed it all—worldwide fame, beauty, money, and a future brighter than her smile. But with no "EV" guiding her life, she dipped into despair and tragically took her own life. So what happened? God knows. And we do know she's not the only one. Thousands of "successful" people have ended up either bankrupt, on drugs, on in a mess. Why is that?

Rick Warren in his book, The Purpose-Driven Life, has the answer: "It's not about us, it's about God."

How simple, clear and direct. But doable? Not quite so for this chica. I still wanted. Lord, I don't want to appear selfish, but I just want to write the best book, the kind that ignites a buzz that's so hot it gives a facelift to Facebook. And secretly, I expected my picture, shining with success and contentment, to be splashed on the home page of my website.

Then Paul dampened my dream. In his bold, direct style, he said: "My counsel is this. Live freely, animated and motivated by God's spirit. Then you won't feed the compulsions of selfishness. For there is a root of sinful self-interest in us that is at odds with a free spirit, just as the free spirit is incompatible with selfishness. These two ways of life are antithetical, so that you cannot live at times one way and at other times another way according to how you feel on any given day..."

...being the obedient chica that I try to be, I changed my thinking. Working to be a best-selling author is about me. Conversely, working hard to bring a message that points readers to Christ, that's about God....

...at the end of the day, when the house is silent—our esposo and ninos are asleep—we put on our soft slippers, slide into our comfy sofa, and ask ourselves: Right now, today this moment, does my to-do list for life align with God's eternal purpose, or does it, instead, satisfy my personal preferences? Do the things I spend the most time, energy and money on have eternal value—significance that will last beyond this world?

If the answer is si, then, from the depths of our soul and sincerity in our heart, we can say: "Lord, I'm in perfect, perfect peace even if this is all there is."

How to Launch a Best-Selling Christian Book | 95

If we are all as honest as Janet Eckles, I think we would agree with her. As Christian authors, we can try, through God's help, to find that balance, and at the same time, bring wonderful Christian books— fiction and nonfiction—to readers who long to read quality books. In fact, with steadfast dedication, relationships formed within the John 3:16 Marketing Network, and following the guidelines I have shared, it is a realistic goal for a debut author to reach best-seller status for one day in a sub-category on Amazon out of seven million plus books.

Most authors start out with dreams of writing one book, but become hooked and continue to write more. The success of a first book inspires confidence, making one feel, well—confident. God can do whatever He wants, but without a way to gain recognition, that "gem of a book" might not be discovered.

In closing, let me ask: **How successful will your launch be if you only know a few people—some church friends and maybe a few writers in your critique group?** You know what to do, but you have to have people in place to help you spread the word about your incredible, awesome, one-of-a-kind book. Even if you have a thousand people on Facebook, your reach will only be one thousand people. What if you have dozens or even hundreds of people who know what you are trying to do and are willing to help you in your book launch?

The possibilities become endless, only limited by imagination, energy, and determination. The John 3:16 Network will be there to help you if you build those relationships and commit your way to the one who makes all dreams come true—and then some. What God does with our books is up to Him. I am glad I can't control that because God always does so much more than I could ask. His ways are better.

Chapter Thirteen
Amazon Creates Another Way for Authors To Make Money Selling e-books - What's the Hype About Kindle Direct Publishing?

The first time I read about Kindle Direct Publishing, also known as KDP, I couldn't see the value of it. Why would I want to give away a Kindle book for up to five days every three months and be forced to yank it off all other distribution sites, including Smashwords? I had three e-books at that time being sold through Smashwords, and with their premium distribution, my books were available to Apple iPad/iBooks, Nook, Sony Reader, Kobo and other websites I learned about later. I didn't understand the fine print about the KDP Loan Option, which sounded like a lot of hype about nothing, and I didn't know anyone who was enrolled. I wrote off KDP thinking it was too much trouble to implement and I would be wasting my time.

While our chief focus is to help Christian authors launch their books when published on Amazon, one of the most valuable aspects of belonging to the network is the sharing of information. In January 2012, we had a new member, Bob Saffrin, who emailed me about his success with a Kindle book, *Moses-Steps to a Life of Faith,* in the KDP Select. After offering it for one day free, he had almost four thousand e-books "sold" and topped the charts in all the nonfiction subcategories.

In over a year of launching books, we had never had anywhere close to that number of books sold in one day—and we are a network that launches books. Of course, Mr. Saffrin's e-book was free, so my next questions was, besides the great exposure he had received—four thousand books loaded on Kindles in the United States and Canada and even other countries sounded awesome—would those downloads translate into royalties? Or was it a fluke?

Many people had bought Kindles for Christmas and were looking for cheap e-books to load on their new "toy."

I started to pay attention to KDP Select through other authors in the John 3:16 Marketing Network. Some were willing to share their numbers. Martin Roth, an Australian author of international thrillers, emailed me about his success with Kindle Direct Publishing. He, too, had "sold" thousands of e-books with KDP. Now I had validation that it wasn't just nonfiction books that were doing well with KDP Select but fiction books also; and it couldn't have been just an after-Christmas rush to upload e-books on new Kindles. This was for real.

I decided to give KDP Select a try—which required a lot of effort on my part. Mr. Roth warned me that it was important to make sure you removed your e-book from all distribution sites except Amazon. Your book had to be exclusive to Amazon. My first thought was, how would they know anyway?

Don't be fooled—Amazon will find your e-book on other websites and contact you to remove it. They are serious about this. When Amazon says exclusivity, they mean it. I waited a couple of months before enrolling my book in the program to ensure it was removed from all websites I knew about, and Amazon found more later and alerted me.

My book *Children of Dreams* is an adoption memoir, and that was the first book I put into the Kindle Direct Publishing Program. In the meantime, some of our John 3:16 Authors had compiled a list of FREE websites where you could promote or advertise your e-book the days it was free on Amazon. I went through that list to maximize my book's exposure.

For two days, over Mother's Day weekend, I offered *Children of Dreams* for free on Kindle. By the end of the weekend, I had almost 17,000 e-books downloaded and it hit number eleven out of all free books on Amazon.

I was ecstatic to have that many books downloaded on Kindles all over the world. In comparison to the number of e-books I had sold previously, it was astounding. The question I had was, how can I make money with this?

Since that weekend, I have offered my other e-books for free through Kindle Direct Publishing. For the month of July, I received a royalty payment from Amazon for $450. Another author in the John 3:16 Marketing Network made $4,000 last month through KDP Select.

The numbers vary wildly, but you can make money using Kindle Direct Publishing. I am delighted to make a few dollars to pay a bill, and the most important thing is I didn't spend a dime hiring a publicist or a marketing firm—and, to be honest, they will soon exhaust anyone's financial resources and may not sell you a single book. I am speaking from personal experience.

Is KDP Select for you? To learn more about the specific details, go to http://kdp.amazon.com/self-publishing/KDPSelect. There are also step-by-step instructions on how to enroll your book.

You might ask, "What about the exclusivity requirement? That means my book can't be sold anywhere else."

Here are my thoughts: If it bothers you, don't do it. Amazon has come up with a marketing method that works. It's a win-win for Amazon and the author. You have a choice, and as long as authors have that choice, I see nothing wrong with it. Amazon is in business and they are good at it. Looking at their growth and market share, they are probably the best. The challenge is for another company to come up with a better "KDP Select" than Amazon's.

Here are some suggestions for anyone who is listening: Implement a similar program that doesn't require exclusivity. Challenge Amazon. Become a bigger player by offering authors more. What about an 80 percent royalty instead of 75 on books priced at $2.99 or more? What about a 50 percent royalty on books that are only 99 cents? What about allowing us to make our books free whenever we want—ten days a month instead of five?

Just like a lover woos his mistress, you've got to convince me to give up KDP Select in its current form and prove that you can offer me something better. The royalty payments I have received from Smashwords pale in comparison to what I have earned with Amazon, even with Smashwords' premium distribution. In fact, the $65 in my Smashwords account isn't enough to deposit into my bank account based on their minimum requirement for direct deposit.

Until another company convinces me otherwise, I will stick with Kindle Direct Publishing, despite its exclusivity. Amazon needs more competition from other companies to entice them to adjust their paradigm. As long as KDP continues to put more money in authors' pockets, Amazon won't have any inclination to "rock the boat" and change it.

One thing I want to stress, however, is you still need to promote your book. Laziness in promotion won't sell books. KDP Select will require effort in terms of letting websites and others know when your Kindle book is free. Then you have the opportunity to make some money after the free promotion is over. It's the uptake in sales following the free promotion that rings up that royalty check.

I believe part of this is attributable to the fact that Amazon takes note when your book ranks high during a free promotion and will advertise it to those who have bought similar books after the free promotion is over. Remember, when you make money, Amazon does, too, so it's in Amazon's best interest to keep promoting your book if it does well on the free promotion. Amazon also pays every month through direct deposit into authors' bank accounts if it's set up that way. My question is, why would anyone not want to do it?

As a final comment, while much of the information in this book is focused on launching a book through the John 3:16 Marketing Network or Christian authors who want to connect with other like-minded authors, **I wanted to help everyone build a stronger Amazon platform.**

I have seen far too many authors not do the simple things that can go a long way towards marketing books cheaply.

Humanly speaking, marketing is a game. Unfortunately, too many people want your shirt, your shoes, and your wallet in the process. The information contained in this book is almost free versus some of the expensive programs that, while good, are out of the financial reach of many authors.

Also, don't forget there are other formats you should attempt to market your book. I also hosted a book give-away on Goodreads. Over four hundred potential readers entered their names for a free print book. I am in the process of contacting all of them individually who did not win a copy to let them know they can download a free audiobook from http://LorilynRoberts.com.

I'm surprised by how many readers have downloaded the audiobook—roughly thirty percent. I'm adding those names to my opt-in reader list. I also noted that nearly all of them listed fantasy, paranormal, and science fiction as their "favorite type books." Note: These readers wanted to win my book. I can't think of a better way to connect personally with future potential fans.

I've been discussing with the administrator of a teen reading group on Goodreads the possibility of *Seventh Dimension – The Door* being picked as a discussion book for their book club. What's most important is these readers represent my "target audience."

Figure out how to reach your select group of people and think creatively in terms of a book launch—it might be something a little different from what I have described here, but don't be afraid to "think outside the box."

Remember, if you are serious about writing and marketing, you can't give up. You are running a marathon, not a sprint. Pick and choose your marketing opportunities wisely, making the most of every opportunity. Draw up a plan that won't exceed your limitations, both in time and money. Acknowledge that what works for someone else may not work for you. Whatever you do, don't give up—give it to God.

The key is to keep "the main thing" the main thing in our relationship with God and others as we pursue our dream of becoming a successful author. Hopefully, what I have shared about the John 3:16 Marketing Network will open your eyes to possibilities you might not have considered—that are eternal in value. **May you find your path in His Word, the Author of the greatest Book ever written. God bless.**

Chapter Fourteen
Where to Meet
John 3:16 Marketing Network Members

Find members and information on our Facebook page: Facebook Christian Book Launches

Twitter Handle @John316Network
#John316Author

Blog and membership list: http://john316mn.blogspot.com
Resource page: http://bit.ly/Rv6ru6
Join: http://bit.ly/jWlYKJ
or
http://bit.ly/e6PGev
.
Forum:
http://groups.yahoo.com/group/John316MarketingNetwork
You will need to be a member to post on the Yahoo forum.

New John 3:16 Marketing Network Launch Page:
http://John316MarketingNetwork.com

Questions? Feel free to contact me at llwroberts at cox.net.

###

Lorilyn Roberts is a Christian author who writes children's picture books, adult nonfiction, memoirs, and a YA Christian fantasy series, *Seventh Dimension*. The first in the series, *The Door* was just published (October 2012).

Ms. Roberts graduated Magna Cum Laude from the University of Alabama for her undergraduate work, including studying in Israel and England. She received her Master's in Creative Writing from Perelandra College and graduated from the Institute of Children's Literature.

Lorilyn Roberts is also the founder of the John 3:16 Marketing Network, a network of Christian authors who are passionate about promoting books with a Christian worldview.

You can visit Lorilyn Roberts at the following websites:

http://lorilynroberts.com
http://lorilynroberts.blogspot.com
http://twitter.com/lorilynroberts

JUST RELEASED!

Read *Seventh Dimension – the Door* and journey where you've never been— an eternal world that will leave you turning the pages— a love story embracing thousands of years in multiple dimensions and realities. *The Door* is only the beginning of this fabulous three-book epic into the present, past, and future.

Praise for Seventh Dimension – The Door

"Dazzling imagery, like a Biblical *Alice in Wonderland*"
Roger Hunt, Roger Hunt Music

"A heartwarming story with loveable animal characters, a stirring heroine, and a king's love for his children—truly pleasing for young and old alike."
Hannah Bombardier, age 17

"A beautiful and meaningful story that keeps you on the edge of your seat!"
Leah Palmer, age 14

"If you enjoyed *The Chronicles of Narnia* by C. S. Lewis, you will love this book."
Bob Saffrin, best-selling author-pastor

"A colorful portrait painted with entertaining characters, lively dialogue, and beautifully adorned with a profound message. The life-like journey evokes tears and cheers, filling the reader with delight."
Janet Perez Eckles, best-selling author

www.ingramcontent.com/pod-product-compliance
Lightning Source LLC
Chambersburg PA
CBHW022102170526
45157CB00004B/1450